WESTIN HOTELS

The Plaza

Designed by Philip Clucas MSIAD

Produced by Ted Smart and David Gibbon

Color Library Books

With special thanks
to the pride of The Plaza
and the joy of its guests:
the people who work so hard
to make it work so well.

*The back-to-back letters that appear on everything from door knobs
(previous page, left) to silver service at The Plaza are the object of more
curiosity among the hotel's guests than anything else about the place.
But the answer to who designed it and why is, unfortunately, lost. Among
the accepted explanations is that it symbolizes the proximity of Central
Park and Grand Army Plaza, which most scholars discount because of
the proof they have that it was designed by someone in Henry
Hardenbergh's architectural firm, if not by Hardenbergh himself. He used
the same symbol in his design for the Copley Plaza in Boston, which
doesn't have a park and a plaza back-to-back. Probably closest to the
truth about the back-to-back P's is the simplest theory of all, put forth by
Paul Goldberger, architecture critic of The New York Times. He points out
that the private clubs that were proliferating at the turn of the century
generally identified themselves with elaborate monograms made up of
their initials. It was clear that Hardenbergh had been asked to design a
hotel with the aspects of a private club, and only natural that he would
follow the custom of designing a monogram to identify it. It is a fact that
he never included a sign with the hotel's name anywhere on the facade
and none was there for many many years. But making a symmetrical
design out of the letter P, which is top-heavy, was a challenge even for the
master builder. Fortunately, French builders had often placed letters
backwards in their designs and Hardenbergh followed their lead, but
with a great classic simplicity that makes it letter-perfect.*

CONTENTS

The Plaza is 75. Eloise is six. Neither of them has any reason to lie about her age, but it should be pointed out that Eloise, one of the most famous in an impressive list of well-known Plaza guests, was six when she checked in at The Plaza in 1955; and a hotel called The Plaza has been overlooking the southeast corner of New York's Central Park since 1890.

The original Plaza Hotel should have been there long before that. Construction of the eight-story building began in 1881 on the site of an ice-skating rink that had provided an outdoor haven for Mrs. Astor's "Four Hundred", close to, but out of elbow-rubbing range of ordinary New Yorkers in the park across the street. The project was held up for eight years because of money problems and was finally finished by an insurance company that had foreclosed on one of its mortgages.

But when it opened in time for the 1890 fall season, everyone agreed it had been well-worth the wait and surely worth the $3 million it had cost.

Though the skating rink had been nice, the neighborhood was changing. Carrie Astor had moved into her new house on Fifth Avenue at 65th Street and fashionable New York had followed her uptown. Cornelius Vanderbilt II had built a little palace facing the asphalt-covered Central Park Plaza and was talking with the great architect George B. Post about making it bigger. It was very clear that upper Fifth Avenue was the place to be, but certainly not the place to have a skating rink.

The hotel was a perfect answer. People of fashion who still lived in less fashionable neighborhoods downtown turned to it as a place to do their entertaining, a thing that simply was not done in New York society before there was a Plaza Hotel.

The 1892 edition of Moses King's *Handbook of New York*, still

The dreams of men like Ben Beinecke gave us today's Plaza on the site of the smaller original.

considered one of the best series of guides ever produced in a city that has had much more than its share, called the original Plaza "one of the grandest hotels in the world".

The following year, King seemed even more excited. "It is one of the most attractive public houses in the wide world", he wrote. "Its front is on the matchless Fifth Avenue, with its unceasing procession of beauty and elegance on the sidewalks and in the line of carriages at the entrance to Central Park, the goal for all fashionable drives."

But location wasn't all that impressed him. "The Plaza hotel to an unusual degree combines beauty and convenience," he said of the original building. "Rising majestically from the broad Plaza to the height of eight full-stories, in brick and brownstone, diversified, but not overladen, with terra cotta and polished marble, balconies and cornices, it shows rich and tasteful effects on all sides and the simple beauty of Italian Renaissance architecture. There is nothing of the narrow tower effect about this broad-based and dignified structure, but its 500 feet of frontage on three streets suggests comfort, rest and security."

Inside, according to King's 1893 *Handbook,* " . . . a large part of the main floor is finished with choice marble mosaic pavements, silvered ceilings, enfoliated bronze columns, counters of Mexican onyx, woodwork of mahogany, and fine paintings. Here are the reception rooms with their Gobelin tapestries; and the great lounging rooms where ladies and gentlemen meet amid Persian rugs, dainty tables, rich easy chairs, costly paintings and other attractive features.

"The pink parlor and the blue parlor, facing Fifth Avenue on the second floor, are furnished in white and gold with onyx tables, delicately

Hotel men as well as the public were given detailed reports that added up to the fact that the new Plaza was truly the last word.

frescoed ceilings and walls finished *en panel* in embossed silk drapery in delicate colors. The great dining-room, 80 by 40 feet, has a graceful arched roof, 30 feet high, rich in frescoes and fretted gold; and is finished in dead white and gold with stained-glass windows and polished oak furniture. The walls are adorned with paintings of the Five Senses, executed in Paris.

"The Restaurant and Café are beautiful and attractive rooms of great size on the 59th Street side; and the bar-room is equipped with onyx

counters and *primavera* furniture. The public apartments are adorned with many paintings of the first order, including Pope's life-like pictures of lions, horses and dogs, and Cowles's 'Shoshone Falls'. There are 400 guest rooms, all of them large and airy, with broad corridors laid with heavy red velvet carpets."

If anyone had told Moses King that this building would be torn down a dozen years later, he'd have had him arrested.

The lion was the original hotel's symbol and representations of the king of beasts appeared everywhere from the mosaic floors to the patterns in the lace curtains that hung in the guest room windows. A painting of a lion by Alexander Pope that was in a place of honor on the main floor was a

Paul Starrett (top) and Walter H. Clough supervised construction with some help from an army of sidewalk superintendants.

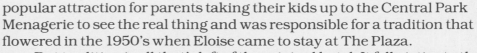

popular attraction for parents taking their kids up to the Central Park Menagerie to see the real thing and was responsible for a tradition that flowered in the 1950's when Eloise came to stay at The Plaza.

But tradition is all that's left of the original hotel. It fell victim to the New York tradition of destroying the old to make way for the new. Fortunately, in the case of today's Plaza, the story has a happy ending. It has a fascinating beginning, too.

'Build me my kind of hotel...'

The people who ran the insurance company that owned the old hotel knew better than to try to operate it themselves and leased the property to professionals for 15 years. All they wanted was to get their money back, and when the George A. Fuller Company offered them $3 million for the property, they could hardly control their excitement. The deal, the biggest cash real estate transaction in the previous history of New York, was made in 1902. From that moment on, the Hammond brothers, who held the lease, had new landlords.

But these people had something more in mind than collecting $10,500 a month in rental fees. They had a dream, and it was clear from the beginning that the building they had bought wasn't nearly big enough to contain it.

The men involved were products of the "American Dream". Each of them had started out with nothing, and here they were in 1902 talking about tearing down a $3 million building and replacing it with something

THE PLAZA
NEW YORK

Fifth Avenue at 59th Street

THE WORLD'S
MOST LUXURIOUS HOTEL

Opened Tuesday, October 1, 1907

RATES

Single Rooms $2.50 per day, with bath $4.00, $6.00
Double Rooms with bath $6.00 to $10.00 per day.
Parlor, Bedroom and Bath $12.00 to $20.00 per day.
Parlor, two Bedrooms and two Baths $16.00, $18.00,
$20.00 and $25.00 per day.

FRED. STERRY, Managing Director

bigger, grander and much more expensive.

One of them was Harry St. Francis Black, chairman of the United States Realty and Construction Company, Fuller's parent company. He had given up a promising career in the general store in his native Coburg, Ontario, to join a surveying party in the Canadian Northwest in the 1870's. He never went back to Coburg. When the surveying was done, he took a job as a "commercial traveler" for a Chicago woolen house with the Pacific Northwest as his territory. It was a virgin territory in those days and Harry was a welcome sight in stores in every part of Washington and Oregon. There was no doubt they needed his wool, but in his travels, Harry noticed another need. There was a lot of expansion going on but not many banks to finance it, so Harry started a couple. It wasn't long before he was traveling for himself.

Harry S. Black (left) kept things moving, while Managing Director Fred Sterry kept moving himself all over the world to find treasures "just right" for the new hotel.

But his life wasn't all work and no play. He took a vacation in 1895 and, fortunately for Harry, so did George A. Fuller, a very successful contractor. Fuller and others were beginning to experiment with steel frame buildings and the idea interested Harry Black. Before the vacation was over, Harry had a new job and a new interest, George Fuller's daughter, Allon Mae.

When he married the girl, he also became vice-president of his new father-in-law's company, a job he probably would have gotten anyway. The marriage lasted less than 10 years, but his association with the company lasted the rest of his life. And through a series of mergers engineered by Black, it became the first construction company that was also an investment company with the ability to finance its own projects.

It was a brand-new company when it bought the old Plaza, and though it had assets of $66 million, Black had chosen to join forces with an outsider to put the deal together.

He was another self-made man named Bernhard Beinecke, who had come from Germany some 40 years earlier without a pfennig in his pocket.

Ben Beinecke's first job in America was as a delivery man for a New York butcher. In an almost classical example of the rags-to-riches story, he saved his money, learned the business and then bought it.

Realizing that the real money in the meat business went to people who sold it to people like him, he soon sold the butcher shop and became a wholesaler. He cultivated hotels and restaurants as customers and in 1876

The skyline has changed over the years. The Savoy Plaza has gone; 9 W. 57th St. has arrived and with it the Park Lane tower. But The Plaza stays serenely unchanged.

managed to get the contract to supply all the meat for the great American Centennial Exposition in Philadelphia.

The Fair was good business for a lot of American businessmen because of the attention it attracted in Europe. It was terrific for Ben Beinecke because meat was one of America's biggest export products in the late 19th century. In a very short time he had sold his company to a group of British financiers and become a financier himself.

Most of his friends and former customers were hotel men, and it seemed only natural for him to invest his money with them. But their ideas usually involved big commercial properties that were clean, comfortable and profitable but not too memorable. Together they built a few, but Ben Beinecke had a different vision. He wanted to build a hotel that would be like a private club. He wanted to build a hotel like The Plaza.

He found the support he needed in the person of Harry Black. But the more they discussed the project, the more they realized such elegance called for big money, more than either of them had. They found their big

money in the person of John W. Gates, one of the richest men in America; a man who, like themselves, had started with nothing.

Gates is the kind of man whose life story is almost too fantastic to be believed. But the truth is that he started life on an Illinois farm and built a personal fortune of well over $100,000,000 before he was 50. And the best part is that he had fun doing it.

He left the farm as soon as he could and got involved in a feed store, which failed miserably. His father-in-law loaned him enough to start a new venture, a hardware store, and young John was on his way.

One day two men from a nearby town came into his store with a new kind of fence wire they had developed. It was strong and it was cheap, it

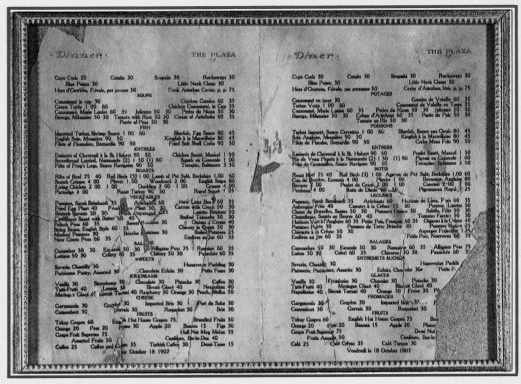

A dinner menu dating back to 1907 shows its age both in prices and its condition. The meals then, as now, were memorable.

didn't pile up snow in the winter nor weeds in the summer and it had little barbs attached to keep curious critters from trying to knock it down.

"Sure, I'll sell it for you," said John, and he packed his bags and headed for Texas where he knew there would be an easy market. Easy for him.

Texas ranchers are a skeptical bunch and even though Gates told them that barbed wire was "lighter than air, stronger than whiskey and cheaper than dirt", it was still a new-fangled invention and they weren't having any. An ordinary salesman would have moved on muttering to himself about having to deal with stupid people. But nobody has ever called John Gates "ordinary".

He went down to San Antonio and built a barbed wire pen in the middle of Military Plaza. He put 50 longhorn steers inside and then went around town betting local ranchers $100 against $10 that the steers couldn't get out. He covered $5000 in bets and then, just to make it more interesting, handed a cowboy a flaming torch and told him to stampede the cattle.

The fence held, the ranchers lost the bet and Gates was in business. Eventually he got control of all the barbed wire patents and almost all the companies manufacturing steel wire. But when his corporation merged with United States Steel, J. P. Morgan refused to give Gates an active role. In fact, very few of the people who made Wall Street run wanted it known that

they ran with the likes of John Gates. He was richer than many of them, and a better businessman. But he had a reputation as a gambler. In the early days he was known as "Betcha a Million Gates", and even though it was finally refined to "Bet a Million", the name stuck with him all his life and it was a name that didn't inspire confidence among potential investors.

The most famous story of his mania for betting on anything at all starts with a poker game in his apartment at the old Waldorf-Astoria. It was raining and Gates noticed the drops of water on the window. "Say John," he said to one of his partners, "see them two raindrops? I'll bet that fellow on this side reaches the bottom before that one over there." First he bet $10 then raised it to $100 and soon everybody in the room was in on the act

The Rose Restaurant, after a brief stint as an automobile showroom, was renovated into the famous Persian Room.

with thousands riding down the windowpane with those two drops of water.

During another of his games, he was told that the head of U.S. Steel was at the door and wanted to talk with him. "Tell him the game is going to be so high it would be over his head," said Gates, and went right on playing.

But Wall Street's distrust notwithstanding, he wasn't a reckless man and he certainly wasn't opposed to stacking life's deck in his favor. When he heard that Black and Beinecke were looking for capital for a new Plaza Hotel, he offered to bet his entire fortune on the project with one condition: They would have to hire a man named Fred Sterry to manage it.

Harry Black's life had taken a dramatic turn when he met George Fuller on a vacation. History was about to repeat itself. He had met Fred Sterry on a trip to Palm Beach and he knew that John Gates was providing him with a lot more than an offer of fresh money.

Fred Sterry grew up in Albany, New York, not far from Saratoga

Springs where he got his first job at the United States Hotel, which is where everybody who was anybody in 19th-century America made it a point to spend at least part of the summer. It was known as "The Baden-Baden of America", and it was a perfect place for a young man to make a name for himself. Before he was 30, Sterry was managing director of the Homestead at Hot Springs, Virginia, and not long after was persuaded to simultaneously manage both The Breakers and the Royal Poinciana, the hotels that put Palm Beach, Florida on the map.

Some historians say that without Fred Sterry's special flair, Palm Beach would be just another winter resort. The fact is, his guests adored him. Among his admirers were Gates, who had known him since his Saratoga days, and Black who once told him he was wasting his time in resorts and really ought to be part of the New York scene.

"Build me my kind of hotel in New York and I'll come," is what Sterry had replied.

It was about to happen. The Plaza would be Fred Sterry's kind of hotel.

'A typical French house'

Choosing an architect to design Sterry's kind of hotel was one of the easiest decisions the partners had to make and it would be hard to imagine a better choice than Henry Janeway Hardenbergh. Two of the directors of the U.S. Realty company, Paul Starrett and Walter Clough, had just finished building the Willard Hotel in Washington and were in the planning stages for the Copley Plaza in Boston, both designed by Hardenbergh. The architect had made a name for himself in New York with his Waldorf-Astoria Hotel on the present site of the Empire State Building and with an apartment building he had designed for Edward Clark of the Singer Sewing Machine Company, the Dakota on the west side of Central Park. A newer building on Manhattan's West Side, the Art Students League on West 57th Street, contained more clues than any of the others about what Hardenbergh would do with the Plaza commission. He would build it in the style of the French Renaissance.

The Plaza's builders were sure the city would stop growing at 59th and Fifth. They never dreamed that skyscrapers would frame their hotel.

The design phase took place during the remaining term of the lease on the old building and the day it expired, in June, 1905, demolition began. The day after that, Fred Sterry went on the payroll and began ordering carpets and tapestries, china and silver. Two months later the old building was gone and New York's sidewalk superintendents started taking bets on how long it would take to build the new one. The contractors said it would be ready in 28 months. The sidewalk superintendents couldn't help grinning.

But Starret and Clough had the last laugh. The Plaza was built, furnished and ready for guests 27 months later, in early fall, 1907. *The New York Times* couldn't believe it. "This is the speed record in the construction of hotels in this city", it said, "and it very likely follows as a corollary in the world".

If the contractors had worked at a fever pitch, so did Fred Sterry. No detail escaped him. "Building a house like this is much like making a woman's dress," he said during a pre-opening tour of the building. "Everything is specially made and specially fitted for a purpose. I will venture to say there is not a stock thing in the decorations. Even the border for the mosaic floor was designed for this room, and that open circle in the bronze work was made for a clock, in turn made for that particular space, and so with the carpets, furniture and tapestries. Quite different from the old style of opening an inn!"

All the furniture in the hotel had been made by the Pooley Company of

Architect Henry J. Hardenbergh may not have known the site would change, but he knew very well his building would always be at center-stage.

Philadelphia whose owner, E. F. Pooley, had also served as a design consultant. What they weren't able to make, they went to Europe to find. They bought linen in Ireland, crystal in France, lace curtains in Switzerland. They bought so much, in fact, the only practical way to get it all to New York was to charter their own ships.

The emphasis was on making the new hotel elegant in the manner of the French chateaux and they surely succeeded. On the hotel's opening day, Pooley drew the prize for understatement when he said: "Mr. Sterry has given New York a typical French house. The Louis periods have been carefully studied and carried out. The whole aspect of the place is cheerful."

To which Fred Sterry added, "We have tried to profit by the experience of others, for in many cases other hotels have been obliged to add improvements after the completion of the hotel that have cost enormous sums."

At that same moment, Harry Black was explaining to reporters why

the $12,500,000 price tag on The Plaza had come out to be about a million dollars over his original estimate. It had nothing at all to do with the handwoven Savonnerie rugs they had placed in the lobbies, nor the three hundred thousand dollars they had paid for silver flatware and candelabra, he told them. All that had been taken into account in the original cost estimate as had the 10 elevators, more than any hotel in the world had at the time, and the five marble staircases. The extra million, he said, went to buy additional land along 58th and 59th Streets.

In spite of Fred Sterry's confidence that improvement would never be necessary, still more land was bought less than 15 years later to build a $2,500,000 annex on the 58th Street side.

The original Tea Room corridor (left) and the 59th St. lobby have changed over time, but the glitter of Plaza crystal is very much alive.

Westin Hotels, which owns and operates The Plaza today, spent more than $33 million in less than six years to rehabilitate the hotel and expects to spend a good deal more.

But if Sterry was wrong in saying that his hotel would never be improved, he had the right idea. The new Plaza was as perfect as perfectionists like himself could make it.

"One more institution has been added to New York's variegated social life," said *The Times.* "The city has gained another showplace. The tourists in the rubber-neck automobiles will have an additional kink put in their necks, and a few more descriptive paragraphs will have to be crowded into the all-around-the-city travelogue of the megaphone cicerone."

The Times could hardly have been more enthusiastic about the opening of the new Plaza: "The design is so successful that the building looms up a welcome addition to the skyline of middle Manhattan. The beautiful simplicity of the exterior is a fitting introduction to the interior. While on all sides there is ample evidence of the lavish expenditure of

money, there is a note of repression that prevails throughout the decorations and furnishings in marked contrast to the gaudy ornamentation to be found in some of New York's large hotels."

But while the design was one of classic elegance, *The Times* pointed out that modern convenience was not forgotten. "Guests will not be worried as to the correct time, nor be bothered with the winding of clocks. In each room there is a magneta clock which is controlled by a master clock downstairs.

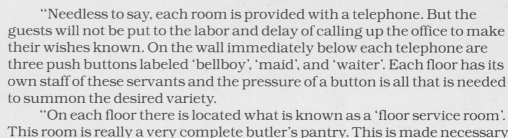

A top-hatted Alfred G. Vanderbilt was first to sign The Plaza's guest register. First day partygoers got free rides in New York's first motorized taxis lined up at the Fifth Avenue entrance.

The photo (opposite page) and the painting (overleaf) are of the hotel's dining rooms since replaced, in part, by the Fifth Avenue lobby.

"Needless to say, each room is provided with a telephone. But the guests will not be put to the labor and delay of calling up the office to make their wishes known. On the wall immediately below each telephone are three push buttons labeled 'bellboy', 'maid', and 'waiter'. Each floor has its own staff of these servants and the pressure of a button is all that is needed to summon the desired variety.

"On each floor there is located what is known as a 'floor service room'. This room is really a very complete butler's pantry. This is made necessary by the fact that many of the patrons who engage suites will have one of their rooms furnished as a dining room. But for those who have only a bedroom and who wish to dine in private, there is in each service room a supply of collapsible dining tables.

". . . No cooking is done in the service rooms, but instant communication is had with the kitchen in the basement by an elaborate

system of electric dumbwaiters. The order for food or drink is put into a pneumatic tube and shot down to a receiving table in the kitchen.

"As soon as a course is prepared, it is put on one of the four dumbwaiters. The man in charge then moves a dial-hand to the number of the floor to which the food is to go, the dumbwaiter then automatically ascends and stops at the proper service room . . . a guest can have his food served as piping hot upon the 15th floor as he can in the main dining room on the main floor.

"To prevent food being purloined from the dumbwaiters while en route, a system of locks has been devised so that once the dial-hand has been pointed at the number of a certain floor and the dumbwaiter started on its way, no other door on that shaft can be opened until the food has reached its scheduled destination."

The 20th century had clearly come to 59th and Fifth.

And there was more to marvel at. Nine steam boilers provided power to run all the machines in the building with enough steam left over to supply the radiators that were in each and every room. Each and every one of those, incidentally, was controlled by its own thermostat. The refrigeration equipment not only produced tons of ice for tea, water and on-the-rocks cocktails, but circulated brine all the way up to the 17th floor to cool a storage room for the safe-keeping of fur coats, blankets and tapestries. Water coming into the building was run through 10 separate filters before it was used, and if it was to be used for drinking or cooking, it was run through still another filter just for good measure . . . in spite of the fact that New York's water supply was the best in the world in 1907, just as it is today.

The building had a built-in vacuum cleaning system, powered by

The Plaza
▽
NEW YORK

steam, and an incredible 17,000 incandescent electric lights kept burning by The Plaza's own dynamos. But for all that, it still looked like a "typical French house," and the whole aspect of The Plaza could indeed be called "cheerful."

The best address in town

Though The Plaza has a French accent, the *Herald-Tribune* once said: "... it is the keystone and the very archetype in the spacious tradition of New York's way of life". It's been true since the day the hotel opened. But, interestingly, of all the people who made The Plaza happen, only Hardenbergh, whose ancestors were among the original Dutch settlers of New Amsterdam, could be called a "New Yorker". And even that would be

This painting is just one example of the love lavished on The Plaza by artists and photographers.

stretching a point. His ancestors disqualified him by moving up the Hudson almost as far as Albany, and he himself was born in New Jersey. Every one of them had come to New York from some other place, proving yet another time that out-of-towners make the best New Yorkers.

Their first guest was a native New Yorker, though. His great-grandfather had been born on Staten Island and had gotten into the transportation business with a little ferryboat he ran between there and Manhattan Island. By the time he died in 1877, he was the most important railroad man in the United States, and that made his son and heir the country's richest man. The owners of The Plaza considered it a very good

sign that Alfred Gwynne Vanderbilt, the old Commodore's great-grandson, was first to sign their register.

Before the day was over, names like Gould and Harriman, Wanamaker and Duke joined the guest list and long before it was over, all the rooms were filled. The best part was that 90 percent of the rooms were filled with permanent tenants. The most expensive suite was rented to John Gates at a rate that was reputed to be somewhere between $35,000 and $45,000 a year. One of the things he got for his money was a private dumbwaiter between his apartment and the basement kitchen.

The Plaza's owners tastefully refused to tell the Press how much their guests were paying for the privilege of living there, which gave reporters an opportunity to guess for themselves. One of the wildest guesses was that, fully-occupied, The Plaza was collecting $387 million a day for its rooms.

Not everyone who streamed through the front door of The Plaza on October 1, 1907 signed the guest register. They were guests of another sort,

Gold frames most of The Plaza's doorways and highlights decorative detail. The morning after opening night, manager Fred Sterry ordered that the gold be covered with shellac so his guests wouldn't be too dazzled.

there for private parties or just to have a look around. But the majority of them were familiar faces to the crowds of people across the street on the edge of Central Park. Diamond Jim Brady was one, but the crowd was distracted from his face by the woman on his arm, no less a person than Lillian Russell. Other actresses came along to add even more glamour. Billie Burke, Maxine Elliott and Fritzi Scheff were among them. People like David Belasco and Oscar Hammerstein, who had helped make them famous, came too. And for the ladies across the street, John Drew put in an appearance. But probably the most interesting face any of them saw that day belonged to Mark Twain, very close to 72 years old by then.

The people outside had something else to gape at. Some of the guests were leaving The Plaza in the new "auto-cabs" that had, not coincidentally, hit the streets for the first time that day. "Auto-buses" had replaced the Fifth Avenue stagecoaches early in the summer, and using automobiles for public transportation was a natural corollary. Credit for the idea goes to a New Yorker named Harry Allen, who also gets credit for originating the term "taxi", to draw attention to a device he had developed called a "taxi-meter", which let riders know exactly what they should pay for a ride.

He bought a small fleet of four-passenger automobiles, painted them

bright red and green, hired uniformed chauffeurs and parked them in front of The Plaza and the Hotel Belmont. The rates the new meters recorded were 30 cents for the first half-mile and 10 cents for each additional quarter-mile. "Somewhat lower rates than have been obtained in this city before," reported *The Times.*

The meters were shut off on that first day and Allen worked the crowd, offering free rides to Plaza guests, people he knew would become his best customers. Twenty years later, a Plaza guest would anonymously buy a car for a New York cabbie so he'd never have to hunt for transportation when he was in town.

Ironically, The Plaza was for a long time one of the only places in the city to find a motorized taxi. The cabs available in other parts of town were still horse-drawn and it was still necessary to put yourself at the mercy of the driver when the time came to pay for the ride. Today there are only 68

From the Ballroom lobby to corridors to the Terrace Room lobby, the detail is rich, the mood is joyous. The ceilings, the walls, even the floors tell you The Plaza is a wonderful place to be.

horse-drawn cabs left in New York and most are stationed outside The Plaza. (Not one is a hansom cab, those high-backed carriages with little trap doors in the roof that keep turning up in the mystery movies, but that's what New Yorkers call them.)

Where society gathered...

Horse-drawn cabs add a touch of the past to the Plaza scene, as does the hotel itself. But though Alfred G. Vanderbilt would still recognize it, The Plaza isn't quite the same today as it was when he moved in. The first difference he'd probably notice would be the entrance on the Fifth Avenue side. In his day the space was occupied by a terrace people called the Champagne Porch. When it was removed in 1921, the *New York World* gave it the send-off it deserved:

"Farewell to the famous Champagne Porch", said the *World's* front-page story. "That exclusive little nook, entwined with rare flowers, extending out toward Fifth Avenue on the east side of The Plaza Hotel, where none but those possessed of sufficient wealth to drink the finest vintage of France in days gone by, is going. It is the last of the widely-known Fifth Avenue retreats of its kind.

"Where once jeweled women and European royalty could be found almost any evening bent over the rarest foods and the finest drinks there is now only dust and broken bricks and the sound of hammers and saws. The Champagne Porch, where the Prince of Wales viewed the splendor of Fifth Avenue's stream of traffic, where small fortunes have passed in payment of dinner checks on a night where society gathered for its most elegant splurges, is doomed. With Prohibition, it became unnecessary, unfrequented, and would not pay for its own upkeep.

"So, in making the 300-room annex to The Plaza, its manager, Fred

The Fifth Avenue entrance replaced the famous "Champagne Porch," (left) and the leaded glass ceiling is gone from the Palm Court, but the elegance they meant is still a Plaza tradition.

Sterry, decided that this tiny spot where only 10 tables sat but which returned in revenue as much in a summer as the entire dining room, owing to the class of patrons, should be abandoned.

"The Champagne Porch was 40 feet long and 15 feet wide. Before the days of Prohibition it was utilized only by parties that made reservations far in advance and from its Oriental rugs to its costly chandeliers, from its rare appointments of tables, chairs and chinaware to the very uniforms its waiters wore, it was furnished with the most expensive materials obtainable. Ordinary dinner patrons were not placed there. Dinners costing anywhere from $50 to $500, according to the number of guests, only were served there. In other words, it was the restricted area of the exclusive hotel.

"Outside the rose and vine-covered posts and pillars of the porch newsboys used to come evenings, peering in at the diners and invariably they went away with substantial coins in their dirty hands. For this was the post where the rich could be found. The boys soon learned its class.

"Champagne flowed there like so much lemonade at a Sunday school

picnic. At $10 or $15 a bottle, the price of a dinner, including the regular food, tips, expenses of cover charges and the like mounted until few but the most plentifully supplied financially ever went there.

"Now it is going. It is already half-torn down. Its furnishings are to be transferred to the new main dining room that will be located in the center of the hotel. The entire east side of The Plaza will be turned into an entrance and lobby. A new dance floor is being installed in the new addition to the southwest side of the hotel that, according to its builders, will be one of the finest in the country.

" 'We wanted to keep the "the porch" in its former condition and serve ginger ale and elderberry juice', Mr. Sterry said, 'but it couldn't be done. We'll try to give them as nice a dance room as we had a champagne room before'."

There was an entrance on the Plaza side in 1907, but it was a minor affair reached through a narrow corridor that cut the dining room neatly in half. The passageway had glass walls that could be removed to unite the dining area, the uptown side of which became the Fifth Avenue lobby, but they were usually left in place because one half of the dining room was reserved for the hotel's permanent guests. Each of them had an assigned table and the corridor kept them "free from the intrusion of transients or

The light standards in the foreground of this view of the Vanderbilt mansion were moved down a flight to become part of the Fifth Avenue entrance (overleaf).

The main lobby (right) has been altered, but Alfred G. Vanderbilt would still recognize it.

simple diners-out", as they said in those days.

A 1907 guest would be right at home in today's Palm Court, which the builders called The Lounge and guests called the Tea Room. It was modeled on the lines of the wonderful Winter Garden in London's Hotel Carlton, but with special touches all its own. The domed ceiling was executed in pastel green and yellow leaded glass for the hotel by Louis Comfort Tiffany. The French-style mirrored rear wall accented arches supported by four marble caryatids, representing the four seasons.

In a building filled with artifacts imported from Europe, it was easy to believe the figures came from Italy. And, in fact, 1907 newspapers reported they had been removed from "an Italian palace". In later years, the story got

better. The sculpture was done in 1598, people said, and the creator was Donato Donati, a pupil of Michelangelo. A nice story, but not true. The Plaza caryatids were made in New York and they were made in the 20th century. In fact, they weren't even made for the new hotel, but were selected from stock on display in a decorator's showroom on Lexington Avenue. They are copies of carvings Donati made for the entrance to the Pisani palace in Carrara, Italy, and that's where the originals are today.

A few days after the hotel opened, they looked down upon young Gladys Vanderbilt, who lived in her father's house across the street, sitting in the Tea Room with Count Laslo Szechenyi, saying "yes" to his offer of

The originals of the Plaza caryatids were made for the Pisani villa at Carara, Italy.

marriage. It was the beginning of still another tradition, courting at The Plaza. It's hard to imagine a more romantic place to do it.

Over the years, a lot of less-than-romantic people have tried to change the Tea Room into something different. But, fortunately for romance, the room isn't much different today than it was in the beginning. The Tiffany ceiling is gone, unfortunately, victim to the removal of the open courtyard above it, and the name has been changed. They began calling it the Palm Court in the mid 1930's.

The main lobby, off 59th Street, was considered unusual in 1907, not because it was completely finished in Italian marble, carefully selected for its beautiful "treeing", but because it had sofas and chairs, an amenity usually found in reception rooms, not lobbies.

There was a separate reception room, of course. Ladies weren't

exp___ _found in hotel lobbies, even if the furniture was custom-made in France. There was a second ladies' reception room off the 58th Street entrance, too, but because the door was intended to be used by the hotel's permanent guests, there was no separate ladies' entrance there as there was on the uptown side.

There was a special entrance for men on the 59th Street side, too. It led to a café and restaurant that was intended to be used by gentlemen only. It

The figures, representing the four seasons, look down at a continual scene of romance... in every season.

was a big, comfortable room with oak wainscot on the walls and a high pitched ceiling supported by heavy cross-beams and trusses. Even though it had an Aubusson tapestry frieze that had been made in France especially for it, the general style of the room was Spanish.

After the 1921 renovation that converted part of the main restaurant into the Fifth Avenue lobby, the "gentlemen only" rule was relaxed, and the room became what it is today, the most romantic restaurant in the City of New York.

The original planners of The Plaza didn't bother giving their rooms special names. This one was called the Fifth Avenue Café by its patrons, and it wasn't until 1955 that it was formally named the Edwardian Room.

Sixteen years later, the room got less formal, much to the dismay of Plaza-watchers, and became known as "The Green Tulip". The 1971 attempt to capture the mood of every other trendy place in town lasted

three years before the management mercifully restored it to its former elegance. It was part of an overall program to bring back the 1907 look, they said, and had nothing at all to do with the fact that New Yorkers despised the place.

As if to prove it, the restored restaurant wasn't renamed the Edwardian Room, but the Plaza Suite. It looked so much like the old Edwardian Room, though, New Yorkers who flocked back to rediscover the joy of candlelight dinners and breakfasts that had changed the way the city starts its day went right on affectionately calling it by its older name.

The Green Tulip provided a valuable lesson in how not to treat a landmark. *The Times'* architecture columnist, Ada Louise Huxtable, was unmerciful:

"It adulterates The Plaza", she wrote, "to look and feel like any number

The original Edwardian Room with its lavish ceiling was for men only. Today it is for pure romance (overleaf).

of other older big city hotels with residual grandeur, cheapened with tricksy restaurants full of familiar and rather loathsome design gimmicks and arch menus and publicity to match. This is meant to appeal, I assume, to a clientele that equates style with novelty and foolish elaboration, and wit with turgid coyness, and for whom the artifacts of the Edwardian era are less familiar than the surface of the moon.

"New rooms such as The Green Tulip, 'on the site of the Edwardian Room' (RIP), are disaster areas. Fortunately, much detail remains, and fake Tiffany glass can be removed. The room could be restored."

Fortunately, it was restored. The light-colored paint was stripped from

the walls, the hanging plants taken down from the windows and the colored glass removed from the doorway. The gazebos and iron railings were taken away and the old tables and chairs brought back.

It's a pleasure to report that New York has lived happily ever after in the splendor of the Edwardian Room at The Plaza.

The Edwardian Room was originally intended to offer the atmosphere of a private men's club where gentlemen could relax with each other. Their 1907 conversations, as in a private club, followed certain unwritten rules, one of which prohibited the discussion of business. They might have talked into the night about a new art form called cubism that a group of young

The mood of the Edwardian Room (left and above) is reflected in the suites above it (above right).

artists including Pablo Picasso had just introduced in Paris. Or they might have discussed the future of Coney Island, for generations New York's number one summer playground, now that a disastrous fire had leveled its biggest attraction, Luna Park. And they might have begun planning a trip to San Francisco now that the Saint Francis Hotel, destroyed the year before in the great earthquake and fire, was ready to open its doors again.

But if they wanted to talk about the forthcoming merger of the Ringling circus with Barnum and Bailey's traveling show or get the inside story on how J. P. Morgan had single-handedly cooled the threat of a depression by locking 125 bankers in his 36th Street office, The Plaza had another men-only room for that.

It was the inner-sanctum at the back of the hotel, the architect's favorite room. It had been built to Hardenbergh's specifications in German Renaissance style. The dark oak in the high wainscoting and the massive

pilasters was imported for it from England. (. . . Where else but New York could there be a German room in a French building finished with British wood?)

The builders called it "the bar room". Newspapers of the day called it "unique", not just because of its grand scale, which was unusual, nor because of the electric fountain in the center, one of the first such contraptions ever made, but because of the bar itself. It was unobtrusively placed between two heavy wooden columns at the back of the room. The carved woodwork behind it was made to represent three huge wine casks, the wall space above them was filled with romantic murals representing three German castles.

There was no mistaking that this room was intended to be used by

The Oak Room with its massive wood carving was originally the bar.

men. And the lure for men of business was six branch offices of large stock brokerage houses located conveniently in the corridors between it and the main lobby. They were said to be the handsomest in the entire city. A mahogany stock board in one of them had cost $1,500.

Not long after Prohibition went into effect in January, 1920, the bar was removed from the end of the room and the adjoining room, also designed by Hardenbergh, was itself converted into a broker's office, to be occupied by E. F. Hutton and Company until the early 1940's. Fortunately, the fumed oak walls and the carved plaster ceiling suited a broker's image very well and when it was reopened as the Oak Bar after E. F. Hutton moved upstairs, it didn't take much effort to restore the room to its original purpose.

Part of that 1940's restoration was the addition of three murals by the American painter Everett Shinn, a member of the "Ashcan School", a turn-of-the-century movement to create realistic cityscapes. They were painted especially for The Plaza, and two of the three show the hotel as it was in the beginning. One represents the Vanderbilt Mansion before it was torn down to make way for the Bergdorf Goodman department store, and another shows Central Park as it would have looked from the hotel on a cold winter night in 1907. The third, the one over the bar, is of the Pulitzer Fountain as it looked when it was first put outside The Plaza.

Each time the hotel was sold after the reopening of the Oak Bar, the Shinn paintings were not part of the sale and each successive owner had to negotiate separately for them. Westin Hotels, the present owner, negotiated for 14 months before actually buying them.

The Oak Room was officially given its name in the early 1930's, but the

Today the Oak Room is one of New York's best restaurants. The Oak Bar with its Everett Shinn murals (overleaf) is in the next room.

bankers and brokers who considered it their private turf never called it anything but the back room. And they tenaciously held to the concept that the back room was their own private preserve.

An idea whose time had come

A few months before The Plaza opened, the Waldorf-Astoria shocked the hotel and restaurant world by announcing it would serve ladies at any hour

in its restaurants. Of course, it was left to the discretion of their headwaiters to decide if a woman was a "lady". Delmonico's Restaurant sniffed that their red velvet rope was always ready to be opened to an unescorted female diner, "if the lady is known to us". But it was well-known that they had turned Mrs. Cornelius Vanderbilt away because they didn't recognize her. The Astor Hotel followed the Waldorf's lead and announced it would admit registered female guests to its dining room, but all others would be turned away. Meanwhile, down on Madison Avenue, women of fashion had banded together to form the Colony Club and made it a big point to ban *men* from its dining room. Their only problem was that the Madison Avenue Baptist Church across the street had prevented them from getting a liquor license . . . to which the club's president responded:

"Our members are not concerned. Drinking adds weight, you know."

The controversy was raging full-tilt when The Plaza opened, but Fred Sterry neatly avoided it by not even raising an eyebrow when unescorted women patronized the Tea Room or the restaurant. As long as they didn't try to invade the Fifth Avenue Café or the back room, his hotel offered the best of both worlds.

The fountain that once bubbled in the Oak Room is gone, but the Terrace Room boasts a beauty.

The world has long-since caught up with the ideas that were beginning to catch on in 1907. But long before it did, The Plaza was leading the way. It took more than a dozen years to open the Café doors to women and 20 more for the Plaza management to "experiment" with the same idea back in the Oak Room.

In the late '40s, it was announced that women would be welcome for lunch in the Oak Room during the summer months. It took a couple of years for them to come in any significant numbers, but once it was clear The Plaza was really trying, female luncheon guests accounted for nearly half the room's summer business. Most of the male customers loved it, but some preferred to take their martinis in the Oak Bar between Memorial Day and Labor Day. It was still a male sanctuary, experiment or no.

The experiment was such a resounding success that the Oak Room was open to both sexes in the early 1950's. But in a bow to the old patrons who resented the change, it was agreed that both the Oak Room and the Oak Bar would be closed to women during the hours the stock exchanges were open.

Everybody was happy. In a way.

By the late '60s it was clear that what was sauce for the goose was going to have to be sauce for the gander. It was also clear that women were going to have to fight for the right. The fight began in the Oak Room.

At high noon on February 12, 1969, three women walked into the Oak Room and sat down at a table. One was Betty Friedan, the writer and president of the National Organization for Women. Her companions were Diana Gartner, the organization's vice president, and a third woman who refused to be identified. The headwaiter told them they couldn't be served until three when the market closed. "We'll wait," they said. They waited about 15 minutes. "It's obvious we're not going to be served," said Miss Friedan, and they left without a fuss.

Meanwhile, downtown in what they called the "East Village" back then, another contingent from NOW invaded McSorley's Old Ale House, a tavern that had been restricting women for 117 years. They had glasses of ale dumped on them for their trouble.

But they made their point. Before long there were no male bastions in New York outside the private clubs. Some died hard. Some just died. But within a year, The Plaza was proud to announce that, on average, more than 10 percent of its Oak Room luncheon guests were women. Many were executives from nearby advertising agencies, retail stores and cosmetic firms who found it a perfect setting for business lunches. Better still, they found they were warmly welcomed by male patrons as well as by the staff.

A Plaza representative met ships at sea to ease the way through customs for guests who wanted to be band-box fresh when they arrived at the hotel.

Where anyone can be a star

If ever a room was designed to appeal to women, the original Plaza ballroom, upstairs over the Oak Room and occupying the entire western end of the building, was one of the best. It was a room full of crystal and gold and touches of Louis XIV, called in one contemporary account "a glorious reproduction of the salons of the old world". But it had a marvelous touch of the new that would appeal to any man interested in the mechanical marvels of the 20th century. It had a magic balcony.

It was fashionable at the turn-of-the-century for women of society to stage "masques and tableaux vivants" both for their own amusement and for the benefit of their favorite charities. Most of the elegant Fifth Avenue houses had tiny theaters for such affairs, a fad begun in the United States by Leonard Jerome, the man who would become Winston Churchill's grandfather. Jerome built a theater on the second floor of the stable next to his Madison Square mansion; not for his wife, mind you, she had taken her three daughters to Europe and didn't seem interested in coming back, but for a young "cantatrice", a professional singer who had caught his eye. His first production there was an extravagant 1863 benefit for Union soldiers wounded in the Civil War. Many of the society women who were his guests, realizing that this presented an opportunity to get into the limelight, encouraged him to do more such shows. Their husbands, aware of Jerome's enthusiasm for fine horses and beautiful women, not necessarily in that order, began building little theaters of their own. And by 1907, no hotel builder would dream of building a ballroom without a stage.

The Plaza stage was the most unusual of them all. Sterry knew he needed one, but he also wanted to be able to get it out of the way when he

didn't need it. The solution was to design the room with a balcony around three sides. One entire side of the balcony would be an elevator that could be lowered to become the stage. It wasn't an easy solution. He wanted the floor entirely clear when the stage was a balcony and he didn't want anything mechanical to be seen. The Otis Elevator Company came to his rescue by putting the machinery inside the balcony. The machine wound chains that were attached to steel beams in the ceiling. They, in turn, were encased in plated brass tubing that telescoped together when the platform was raised. When it was used as a balcony, it was locked in place by sliding steel beams. Radio City Music Hall in all its glory never boasted a stage as wonderful as this one. It could be raised or lowered in ten seconds with the push of a button.

From its first season, the Plaza ballroom provided *the* stage to appear upon. One of the early productions was "Mrs. Van Vechten's Divorce Dance", starring Mrs. George Gould. *The Theater Magazine* reported that she was "startlingly beautiful, in a wonderful creation of gray satin embroidered in pearls with a sweeping train of point lace". Then the magazine's reporter sighed, ". . . The setting and costuming of these private theatricals is often the professional's admiration and despair, for no expense is spared and no scenic triumph of the artist's creation is beyond their reach."

Money was indeed no object. In fact, if they had given the cost of their

Karl Bitter's sculpture on the Pulitzer Fountain once turned her back on the Vanderbilt mansion. On purpose, many said.

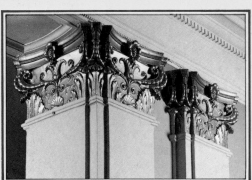

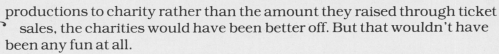

productions to charity rather than the amount they raised through ticket sales, the charities would have been better off. But that wouldn't have been any fun at all.

A masque sponsored by the Junior League in the Plaza ballroom raised $10,000. *The Theater Magazine* reported that the production "would have done credit not only to their elders in society, but to most professionals".

"Nathan Franko's orchestra furnished some quaint old music and the woodland setting at the end of the Plaza ballroom was most effective," reported the magazine. "Miss Mary Hasell made a very lovely Venus and

*A perfect place for a
party! Or a fashion
show. The Terrace Room.*

the dancing of the Dryads was quite the daintiest thing on the program . . . After the masque, a 'divertissement – Les Chansons Bergerettes de Weckerlin', consisting of French songs and dances was given. Nor did the young people stop with these two successful features of the program. The Mistress of the Revels announced that there would be a comedy enacted whose scene was laid three hundred years in the future, and forthwith is

The Plaza has always been perfect for any special occasion. From the original 58th St. restaurant (above) to today's suites or the fabulous Terrace Room (overleaf).

produced an adaptation of Oscar Wilde's 'The Importance of Being Earnest'. After the performance, the masquers mingled with the audience, very attractive in powder and dainty costume."

It wasn't just a young woman's game, either. Society matrons were just as enthusiastic about performing in public, and one of the most lavish productions ever staged at The Plaza was a series of tableaux arranged by, of all people, Mrs. Waldorf Astor, who put on the show to raise money for poor mountaineers in her native Virginia.

All the best people participated and the hit of the day was Mrs. Benjamin Guinness as an Oriental Queen. She wore a huge crown of diamonds on her head and nine ropes of pearls around her neck. Her ears were covered with jeweled discs. It was reported that "no artist has ever graced the stage with an attire that represented the fortune comprised in this costume."

Mrs. Astor provided a touch of professionalism by hiring Mme. Cavalieri of the Metropolitan Opera Company to supervise the makeup and, for her part in the show, she brought in the Metropolitan's ballet master to supervise the steps and gestures of her own pantomime. It turned

Cinderella would be at home here. The clock over the Fifth Avenue door would tell her when to scamper down the Ballroom stairway.

out that she was upstaged by Mrs. James Eustis who appeared in her tableau with a live boa constrictor around her neck.

The entire production was supervised by the world-famous actress Mrs. Patrick Campbell. Mrs. Campbell had already made history at The Plaza. Twice.

A little hideaway downstairs

Mrs. Patrick Campbell was one of the first guests at the hotel, having come from Europe to appear in a Broadway production of Hedda Gabler. Her constant companion was a 17 year-old monkey-spitz poodle, who was both blind and feisty. The month-old Plaza didn't have a policy about whether to allow dogs in its rooms, but Mrs. Campbell made Fred Sterry come up with one on the spot. They would, they did and they still do. The next time Sterry

saw Mrs. Campbell, she was lighting a cigarette in the Tea Room.

When he protested, she stared him down and said, "I have been told this is a free country. I will do nothing to alter that fact."

Sterry told her that he was aware of the fact that women were permitted to smoke in European restaurants. "But," he said, "to do it here is another matter. The Plaza does not wish to be first to permit the custom."

Mrs. Campbell was what is called in polite circles "frank and outspoken," and was very unpopular with the Press, even if she did make good copy. The resulting publicity was very good for The Plaza, very bad for her. And there was plenty of it all over the country.

Actually, she was six weeks ahead of a trend. On New Year's eve, 1907, Café Martin, one of the most popular restaurants in the "White Light District," as Broadway was called, announced that it would allow women to smoke if they wanted to. They did. Some of them did it as early as 11 o'clock! It was the biggest news story of the first day of 1908. Except for one: the story of the first New Year's Eve at The Plaza.

When he confronted Mrs. Campbell in the Tea Room in November, Fred Sterry was already knee-deep in preparations for the New Year's gala, and reservations were already pouring in. By opening the doors between the restaurants and combining them with the Tea Room, he could accommodate 2,500 dinner guests. 6,000 showed up.

By the time Mrs. Stuyvesant Fish arrived, it was impossible to get through the crowd. Every available employee was rounded up and she was escorted to her table by a flying wedge of bellmen. Eventually a resourceful guest discovered she could get into the dining room through the pantry and latecomers followed her lead. People without reservations were held back by a silk and velvet rope, but most of them refused to leave the hotel and stayed until midnight when the orchestra brought everyone to their feet with the playing of "The Star-Spangled Banner" and "Auld Lang Syne."

When the music stopped, the crowd noticed an impressive figure near the orchestra. "Caruso! Caruso!," they shouted. "He is going to sing!" But the great tenor wasn't giving out free samples. "I sing. I sing," he said. "But I sing later."

"Later" turned out to be two weeks later when he made his season début at The Met.

Six thousand may still be a record for the number of people at a Plaza party, but even that early in its life, the hotel staff had mastered the art of handling crowds. Almost from the first day there had been a steady stream of New Yorkers who went there to be seen and to see who else was there. In 1908, the *New York World* published a put-down of the custom in a feature article with the caustic headline: "Bussing Up Fifth Avenue and Dropping in at The Pa-La-Za".

". . . I made my way into the Home-For-The-Incurably-Opulent through the taxicab entrance on the plaza," wrote the *World*'s emissary. "The stream of humanity seemed to be flowing to the right and downward, so I followed the general trend. The staircase turned suddenly, and then what seemed to be a tremendous operating room was before me!

White – nothing but white! Severely, sickeningly, suggestively white! White tables, white tiling, white chairs!

"And people could smile in such a place!"

They had a lot to smile about. What she had stumbled upon was the famous Plaza Grill Room. It was white all right. The only touch of color, except for the bronze light fixtures, was the Delft-blue leather covering the chairs and settees. The effect was intentional. Downstairs grills were popular in hotels of the day. It was also popular to finish them in tones of gray and brown, probably to cut the cost of keeping them clean. Fred Sterry

A good hotel is more than a great place to sleep. Which is why The Plaza's guests agree it is something much more than a good hotel.

wanted to show that he had nothing to hide.

This room had more to show than other grill rooms around town. It was the only one that had a glass-fronted refrigerator that allowed guests to select their own steaks or chops that would be cooked to their order on a six-foot solid brass electric broiler also out in plain sight. The broiler was what a manufacturer today would call "the state of the art" in electric cooking. The company that made it wasn't given to such clichés, but was

The Terrace Room's beauty extends out. And up.

proud to say that their range ". . . will cook perfectly a steak in from five to ten minutes, without scorching, perfectly conserving all the pieces." It was capable, they said, of delivering "twenty-five individual orders of steaks, chops, etc., in one hour."

In the 1920's, the Plaza Grill became something much more than the best place in town to go for a steak. It became the social center for a whole generation of young people . . . the one Gertrude Stein called "The Lost Generation," a group immortalized by Ernest Hemingway and F. Scott Fitzgerald.

Describing New York at twilight during those years when the cocktail hour had been made illegal, Fitzgerald once wrote:

"Through the gloom people went to tea. On all the corners around The Plaza Hotel, girls in short squirrel coats and long flowing skirts and hats like babies' velvet bathtubs waited for the changing traffic to be suctioned

67

up by the revolving doors of the fashionable grill."

A dance floor had been added by then and the lure for the young was a Plaza innovation called tea dancing. It made the grill a great place for boys from Princeton and Yale to meet girls from Vassar and Bryn Mawr and for a dozen years or more it was as important to that generation of young people as any disco became in the '70s for another young generation. And all the elements were just right. The goal of any young generation is to shock the older one, and here they had a pure white room in a hotel that represented the ultimate in elegance. And if they couldn't drink there, they could dance, which was something their grandparents, at least, found quite shocking. It was a perfect arrangement as far as the hotel was concerned, too. The room was in the basement where the revellers could be kept out of sight and out of earshot . . . except when the conga lines got long enough to extend up the stairs through the lobby and out into the street . . . so other guests weren't usually disturbed. And the tea dances took place well before the dinner hour, by which time the dancers had paired off and headed for places like Greenwich Village where the fine art of tavern-keeping was being kept alive for future generations.

In 1947, The Plaza celebrated its 40th anniversary by changing the Grill Room into something more contemporary called The Plaza Rendez-Vous. Where the old room had been stark white, this one was done up in combinations of purple, orange, yellow and red. A garish combination? Believe it or not, it worked! It was designed in three parts

The basement Grill Room was originally a place to get a perfect steak. It became a place for a perfectly divine evening on the town.

with a small cocktail lounge out front. The main room featured a dance floor and a smaller room in the corner featured pure romance. As if concerned that Prohibition might come back, the Rendez-Vous didn't have a bar. Cocktails were served from little rolling carts, another Plaza innovation that became popular in other hotels and restaurants for a while.

The most expensive drink the portable bars dispensed back in 1947 was 25-year-old Grant's Ancient Reserve, imported from Scotland especially for The Plaza. It cost $1.25.

Twenty years later, when supper clubs had gone out of style and cabaret theaters had come into vogue, the old Grill was given another new paint job . . . all red this time . . . and became a cabaret called PLaza 9-. In the late 1970's it was converted into Cinema 3, one of the most comfortable small movie theaters in Manhattan.

Looking at The Plaza from the Park or vice versa is an unforgettable pleasure. The iron gates that once enclosed the Vanderbilt mansion are now a part of the Park at the Conservatory Gardens on Fifth Avenue and 105th St.

A site unrivalled in New York

When the theater was added, the New York City Landmarks Commission, which has an important say in such matters, ruled that there should be enough lobby space so that lines of moviegoers wouldn't appear on the sidewalk outside. But if people don't form long lines outside The Plaza, the sidewalks around it are the very best in the city for people who enjoy people-watching.

It was intended that way. When Calvert Vaux and Frederick Law Olmstead presented their 1858 "Greensward Plan" that would become Central Park, it included a small rectangular area at the southeast corner to give traffic entering the park a place to line up without blocking traffic on the outside streets. The southwest corner, the intersection of Broadway and

Eighth Avenue became a circle and so the lower Fifth Avenue corner became New York's first public plaza. But that was as far as the Greensward Plan went. Olmstead and Vaux were preoccupied with the park itself. They had swamps to drain and lakes to dig; there were bridges and roads to be built, hills and valleys to be created and five *million* trees, shrubs and vines to be planted.

The original plan called for 18 gates to the park, each with a gatekeeper who made sure citizens didn't use the park except during the hours it was officially open, usually from six in the morning until nine at night. Each of

them was given a name, and the entrance at Fifth Avenue and 59th, across from The Plaza, is still officially called the Scholar's Gate.

When Olmstead and Vaux had their backs turned in the park, the architect Richard Morris Hunt, who gave us the main facade of the Metropolitan Museum of Art, submitted plans for making the gates formal affairs "worthy of a great city". The most elaborate of them would face The Plaza where he envisioned a huge fountain. He proposed an entrance to the park's east drive that would be flanked on the west by a 100-foot semicircular terrace dominated by a 50-foot column bearing the seal of the City of New York. At the base of the column would be allegorical sculpture representing the Hudson and East Rivers and a figure of Henry Hudson standing on the prow of a ship. It would have real water, too, in the form of cascades down the hill into the park and then into a basin that held a statue of Christopher Columbus. The basin would drain into the pond that was already there.

But that wasn't the sort of thing the park's designers had in mind at all. Fortunately, the park's commissioners agreed with Olmstead and Vaux's vision that the park should not contain anything that showed the hand of

man and Hunt's scheme was never carried out.

There have been architects and builders trying to put their mark on Central Park since the day it opened. And sculptors. Olmstead and Vaux could get violent on the subject of sculptors.

". . . The park is not a place for sepulchral memorials," read one report, "it is for recreation and pleasure; its especial aim and object is, by all justifiable means, to dispel from the mind of visitors, once inside its enclosure, thoughts of business and memories calculated to sadden and oppress. It is a pleasure ground. The beautiful cemeteries in the vicinity of the city offer abundant opportunities to commemorate, by appropriate memorials, the virtues of those who are passing away."

They didn't always win, of course. There are more than 80 monuments in the park today. But they fought the fight anyway, and one of their most memorable battles was with a giant named Augustus Saint Gaudens over his last and surely greatest work, his equestrian *General Sherman.*

Saint Gaudens had begun the work in 1892, finally finishing it in time to win a gold medal at the 1899 Paris Salon. He apparently wasn't as

impressed as the Parisian judges because when it came back, he completely remade the Victory figure that leads the general's horse. Then he sent it off to Buffalo to be shown at the Pan-American Exposition. After that he cast it in bronze, gave it three coats of gold leaf and announced it was ready to be shipped to New York where it would be given a place of honor on Riverside Drive in front of Grant's Tomb.

"That's what you think!" said the Grant family, horrified at the thought of being upstaged by another Civil War general.

It was strongly urged that the statue be placed at the point where Broadway crosses Seventh Avenue, "between two great currents of traffic, among men and buildings, not among trees." But Saint Gaudens preferred trees to Times Square and requested that the general be placed in the middle of the Mall in Central Park.

The Park Commissioners talked him out of that idea in favor of the still empty plaza above 59th Street, and that's where Sherman finally came to

rest on May 30, 1903. Ironically, trees had been planted in the plaza by then and had to be cut down to make the monument visible.

The part of the plaza below 59th Street and in front of the hotel was nothing more than a mini-park until 1913 when Joseph Pulitzer left $50,000 in his will to build a fountain there. Karl Bitter, the sculptor who had the commission to do the statue of Pomona, Goddess of Abundance, that crowns it, suggested that the entire plaza from 58th to 60th Street

When The Plaza was new, there were sheep in the Park's Sheep Meadow and no sculpture on the Mall. The Park is different today (overleaf) but no less exciting.

ought to be redesigned as a single unit to accommodate both the fountain and the Sherman memorial. That work was done by Thomas Hastings of the architectural firm of Carrere and Hastings, who had done the New York Public Library at 42nd Street and the Frick mansion at 70th Street. His design involved moving the general 16 feet closer to the hotel and placing Pomona in a position (many said intentionally!) with her backside pointed at the Vanderbilt house.

For all that work, no one thought to give the plaza a formal name. It had been known as Central Park Plaza since the beginning, but it wasn't until 1923 that it was officially named Grand Army Plaza in honor of the Union army of the Civil War. They probably needn't have bothered. People went right on calling it what they had always called it: "the plaza".

The Vanderbilt mansion that had framed it on the downtown side went into history in 1928 to make way for the Bergdorf Goodman store, but it left a memorial in the form of the gate that had faced the plaza. It was moved up Fifth Avenue and placed in front of Central Park's Conservatory Gardens at 105th Street.

There is nothing left of the Hotel Savoy that had stood on the other side of Fifth Avenue until it was demolished that same year to make way for McKim, Mead & White's more magnificent Savoy-Plaza Hotel. Nothing is left of the Savoy-Plaza, either. It was replaced in 1968 by Edward Durrell Stone's monster General Motors Building. New York is that kind of town.

"There are certain sites in all the world's great cities that cannot

retrograde," said an early Plaza brochure. "They are fixed and unalterable landmarks of the municipalities in which they are located. They will always be central, even though extensive changes occur in their immediate vicinity. Such is the site of The Plaza, a site unrivalled in New York and unsurpassed in the capitals of Europe . . . New York, confined between its two rivers, cannot expand in every direction as do the cities of Europe. It can only advance northward . . . Gradually the tide has flowed northward mile by mile until it has reached 59th Street, and here it has stopped, permanently, it is believed."

There are hundreds of thousands of New Yorkers living north of 59th

Augustus St. Gaudens' great General Sherman was already part of the scene when the hotel was built. Today it's hard to imagine one without the other.

Street who would question the writer's ability to predict the future, but not many who wouldn't agree that 59th and Fifth still is what the brochure claimed it to be, "the center of the Island of Manhattan."

Fortunately, all the change that has taken place in The Plaza's neighborhood hasn't been bad. The Sherry-Netherland Hotel across 59th Street from GM's marble box arrived on the scene in 1927 adding a wonderful touch to the skyline with its slender lantern-topped tower. Two years later, the same architects, Schultze & Weaver, added the Pierre Hotel's huge mansard roof to the top of the wall of buildings that frame the plaza.

Stanford White's building for the Metropolitan Club, on the 60th Street corner between the two hotels, preceded The Plaza by 14 years, but the fabulous old Knickerbocker Club at the 62nd Street corner, the work of

Delano and Aldrich, arrived on Fifth Avenue seven years after the hotel.

After the park was built, Fifth Avenue above the plaza became a natural magnet for the super rich who competed with each other to see who could build the most palatial mansions. Names like Fish and Phipps, Stuyvesant and Havemeyer began appearing on little brass plates beside the doors of new houses for two miles up the avenue. Some of the houses are still there, of course, but most have been replaced by apartment buildings that, while palatial themselves, weren't at all what the rich and powerful had in mind when they claimed upper Fifth Avenue as their own. The building of The Plaza hotel was one of the things that helped change their minds.

The first apartment building in New York was at Third Avenue and 18th Street, built in 1869. Apartments that followed it, including Hardenbergh's Dakota, were more like today's hotels than today's apartment houses, and though it wasn't difficult finding tenants for them, New Yorkers had always lived in private houses and they were skeptical about sharing the same roof with other families. Besides, if you were rich, how would anybody know it unless you could build an elegant house to prove it? When The Plaza was built, New York's gentry had their alternative. And if living in someone else's building was good enough for the Goulds and the Vanderbilts . . . well, why not?

Three years after The Plaza, McKim, Mead and White built 998 Fifth Avenue at 81st Street, the first apartment house in the row of mansions. It

The views from the upper floors of The Plaza have changed over the years, too.

was only a matter of time before the character of the avenue would change again. Fortunately, the apartment house builders would have two benchmarks to follow, The Plaza and 998 Fifth.

There were die-hards, of course. Fifth Avenue hadn't seen the last of its palace-builders. It was about to see the prize-winner for one-upmanship, a multi-millionaire named Henry Clay Frick.

Frick was a Pennsylvanian who had made a fortune selling coke, the special coal that fuels steel mills. Later he threw in his lot with Andrew Carnegie to parlay his fortune into something like $80 million. But he and

Carnegie weren't what you'd call pals. When Frick saw the house that Carnegie built on upper Fifth Avenue, he decided on the spot to build a place that ". . . will make Andy's look like a miner's shack."

He became single-minded about it. Buying the whole block front on Fifth Avenue between 70th and 71st Streets, he hired Thomas Hastings to design a Florentine palace, society decorator Elsie deWolfe to buy the furnishings and Sir Joseph Duveen to fill it with works of art. When it was finished in 1914, Carnegie ran up a flag of truce. But Frick, satisfied he had won the battle for opulence, ordered a message sent back to his old partner: "Tell him I'll see him in hell, where we are both going."

Plaza interiors have been altered over the years and refurbishing never stops. But through it all elegance has never ever been sacrificed.

Both their mansions still survive, both as art museums. But Frick was clearly the winner. His name is still on that little brass plate out front.

The Plaza is my home

Lord Duveen, the man who built the Frick art collection, lived at The Plaza and, though he had a gallery nearby, he used the Plaza ballroom as the setting for important auctions. Andrew Mellon was his best customer, but he'd provide Old Masters for anyone willing and able to pay for them. "When you pay high for the priceless, you're getting it cheap," he told his customers and the robber-barons lined up for the privilege. It's because of him that there are probably more great works of art in America than in Europe where they were created. And many of the deals that brought them here were made at The Plaza.

Duveen's Plaza apartment was one of the corner suites overlooking both the park and the plaza. Beginning with the super-elegant State Apartments on the first floor, similar suites filled the 59th Street corner on 11 floors. Though they were designed to be easily expanded or contracted, the typical arrangement included a sitting room and dining room reached by a private hallway and three bedrooms, each with its own bath. But if a permanent guest preferred something more spacious, the system of private hallways allowed every room on any side of the floor to be interconnected for anyone who might be able to afford it.

Each of the suites also included private service rooms so that food could be brought in from outside without disturbing the guests in the living quarters.

Special touches were added to give the suites "the luxurious atmosphere of a fine New York residence." All the rooms were finished in Louis XV-XVI style with crystal chandeliers and carved plaster ceilings. There was no wallpaper on any of the walls because Fred Sterry believed plain painted walls in soft tones of gray, cream, yellow and rose had a more soothing effect. For the same reason, there were no pictures on the walls,

either. He achieved a decorative effect with paneling and plaster molding. The woodwork was walnut, pine or mahogany and the furniture was made of the same woods to give a harmonious effect.

And, as advertised, each room had its famous "Magneta" clock. "These clocks keep absolutely correct time," said the manufacturer, "so there will be no excuse for guests who miss a train or lose an appointment." They were controlled by a master-clock in the telephone room and were guaranteed to be completely noiseless. What they meant by "noiseless" was that the electric clocks didn't tick. But they did make a funny buzzing sound.

Enrico Caruso didn't think the sound was funny at all. When the one in his Plaza suite interrupted his practicing, he did what any temperamental tenor would do. He attacked it with a knife. It stopped the noise, but it also

The Magneta Clock, which automatically controlled all the hotel's clocks was a wonder of the age in 1907. Something more than just a pretty face.

stopped every other automatic clock in the building and hundreds of Plaza guests had an excuse to miss a train or lose an appointment.

All the suites were equally endowed with touches of comfort, convenience and elegance, but first among equals was the impressive first floor suite which had just a touch more of everything including a Steinway concert grand piano designed in the Louis XIV style especially for it. It also had access to a private dining room big enough for 200 guests and it was just a short jaunt from there to the ballroom discreetly removed from it at the back of the floor.

The State Suite became home for the late S. R. Guggenheim, who broke Fred Sterry's old rule about having no pictures on his walls. Guggenheim loved modern art and he collected the best. When he moved to The Plaza he brought along his collection of paintings by artists like Matisse and Chagall, Seurat and Klee and no one complained at all when he displayed them on those baroque walls.

The paintings that hung at The Plaza now hang at the Guggenheim Museum up the street, a building that is as far removed from The Plaza's style as any building could possibly be. But, interestingly, some of the work on designing it took place in another Plaza suite.

When Frank Lloyd Wright came to New York to work on the Guggenheim, his only building here, he chose to stay at The Plaza. "It's

genuine. I like it almost as much as if I'd built it myself," he said.

During his stay, he was instrumental in convincing the hotel's owners that the Oak Room was a treasure that shouldn't be touched. But just so no one would get the idea he was a sentimentalist, he told an interviewer:

"The Plaza was built by the Astors, Astorists, Astorites, Vanderbilts, Plasterbilts and Whoeverbilts who wanted a place to dress up and parade and see themselves in great mirrors. So they sent for the finest master of German Renaissance style, Henry Hardenbergh, and he did this – a skyscraper, but not the monstrous thing the skyscraper was to become later. He still managed to keep it with a human sense. There were Ravenna mosaics in the floor, but they covered them up with rugs. A lot of it has been

The dining room, bedroom and parlor of the original State Suite reflected "the elegance of a private dwelling."

spoiled by inferior desecrators – but The Plaza is my home."

He was right about the mosaics in the floor. Each of the main floor rooms had mosaic floors, especially beautiful in the borders. The original designers were the ones who covered them with rugs, expensive rugs by the way, to add a touch of warmth and of quiet. Their intention was to remove the carpets in the summer, which wasn't often done. The best-preserved of the original floors is in the Oak Room, the one Wright was talking about, which has been kept in its original condition because it has

The rooms, including the former drawing room, are now available for special private occasions, (above top and overleaf).

always been kept covered.

But when The Plaza is your home, you're entitled to take more than a casual interest in it. In the beginning, almost everybody who stayed there lived there, but there are only about a dozen permanent guests now, including one who was among the original guests in 1907.

Over the years, Plaza people have made headlines, provided grist for gossip columns and given other New Yorkers interesting conversation-starters.

The stories range from the one about the 1908 guest who decided to dispatch a telegram on her way back from the hotel safe and left $100,000 worth of jewels on the counter . . . where they were still sitting an hour later when she remembered where she'd left them . . . to that of Mrs. Benjamin Kirkland who sent her Boston bulldog to the safe each night to collect her jewels. They include the story about a dowager who never left the hotel in the 19 years she lived at The Plaza, but who did leave standing orders for her chauffeur to bring her Rolls Royce around promptly at nine each morning in case she had some place to go.

They include the tale of Hetty Green, who lived at The Plaza for a month in 1908, possibly the only month she really "lived" in her entire life. Hetty was one of the richest women in the world and she dedicated her life to hanging on to every dime. She lived with her children in a tenement in Hoboken, New Jersey, and commuted to Wall Street each day, always wearing the same dress, to count her money.

Hetty had a daughter who needed a husband. The poor thing was 37 years old and without a prospect. It was a dilemma that melted even Hetty's heart. Her answer was to rent a suite at The Plaza and see what might turn up. To set the stage, Hetty even bought a new dress and spent an afternoon in a beauty parlor. The stage itself was a 10-course dinner party in the suite with (gulp!) no expense spared. Fortunately, she only had to do it once. Among the guests was an elderly bachelor with roots in the Astor family who couldn't resist the young lady's charms and in a few weeks proposed that they get married.

That was the signal Hetty had been waiting for. "I've paid off my daughter's social debts," she announced, and checked out. Her month at The Plaza gave her a taste of a much better life than she had been leading, though. Instead of going back to her Hoboken flat, she moved to the Hotel St. George in Brooklyn Heights, which also had the advantage of being a less-expensive commute to Wall Street. The St George's records show that she never, ever, called for room service.

On the opposite side of Hetty Green's coin, the prize for flamboyance goes to Princess Lwoff-Parlaghy, who in addition to being a princess (a title she picked up from her ex-husband, a Russian prince) was one of the most popular portrait painters in the world at the turn of the century. She had painted the likeness of Germany's Kaiser Wilhelm no less than six times and by the time she checked into a $3,000 per month Plaza suite in 1908, she had done portraits of the Czar the Czarina of Russia, the King of Denmark, the King of Italy, the Queen of Rumania and the Grand Vizier of Persia.

The State Suite also included a custom-made Steinway (above). But for public "Musical Mornings," the Tea Room was the place to be seen (left).

Naturally, important Americans were more than eager to join such company, and people like Andrew Carnegie, August Belmont, Chauncey Depew and New York's mayor, Seth Low, had their portraits painted in the princess's Plaza apartment. They were joined by Robert De Forest, president of the Metropolitan Museum, and Supreme Court Justice Joseph Choate whose Lwoff-Parlaghy portrait is in the collection of the American Museum of Natural History.

The Press reported that her annual income was more than $1 million. She didn't deny it. In sweet Hungarian-accented tones she told them it was hardly possible for her to spend more than $250,000 in any year. But she tried hard.

If the princess had a fatal flaw, it was her love for animals. She had a collection in Europe that included bears, wolves and monkeys, but to the relief of the Plaza staff, left them behind when she went to New York. She did have a little dog with her when she arrived, a spaniel named Bübchen. She had two horses, too, but was content to board them in a stable near the park. Then one day someone took her to the circus and the princess fell in love.

The object of her affection was a lion cub and she announced on the spot that she had to possess him. Fred Sterry was pleased to hear the next day that the Ringling Brothers had turned down her offer to buy the lion, but he probably knew she wouldn't let it end there. She didn't. The subject of her latest portrait, the former Civil War General, Daniel Sickles, agreed to become her agent in the matter and was so influential that the circus owners offered to give him the beast. They finally agreed to let him pay a token $250 and turned the affair into a million-dollar publicity stunt.

Her neighbors in The Plaza were not amused, but Sterry reassured them by requiring the princess to rent a separate room for the lion and to hire a trainer to keep him in check. Except for the one time the animal, whose name was General Goldfleck Sickles, escaped into the third floor corridor, Plaza guests were generally unaware that there was a lion in their midst.

He lived there about three years and then, quite suddenly, Goldfleck died. He was buried, after an elaborate funeral at The Plaza, along with his collection of toys in a pet cemetery north of the city in Hartsdale. His grave is marked by an elaborate stone with the inscription: "Beneath this stone is buried the beautiful young lion Goldfleck whose death is sincerely mourned by his mistress, Princess Lwoff-Parlaghy, New York, 1912."

If people like the princess made good newspaper copy, thousands of celebrated people have stayed and lived at The Plaza confident that their privacy would be respected.

Ferenc Molnár, the Hungarian playwright and novelist who wrote the story that became the musical *Carousel*, became a Plaza resident in 1939. He summed up what it meant to him in an article in which he called The Plaza "a citadel, a fortress for all of us who live here". He went on:

"I have a sense of quiet security, solidity and steadiness when I come home to this mighty edifice with its wide open, free space about it.

"One of Europe's greatest, the late Maurice Maeterlinck lived here under the same roof with me for eight years – but it took me three years to find that out.

"Someone here looks after not only the comfort of the guests but also their privacy."

Bridges across the generation gap

At one point in The Plaza's history, privacy and comfort seem to have gone out of the window. Fortunately, it was all a piece of fiction and the worst effect it had on Plaza guests was that they were captivated by a six-year-old named Eloise.

Though she invaded The Plaza as far back as the 1950's, there are very few New Yorkers today who don't automatically say "Eloise" when the hotel's name is mentioned, and there aren't many guests who need to be told who the little girl is in the oil portrait that hangs in the corridor across from the Palm Court.

Eloise sprang to life in Las Vegas in 1948. She was created as a tension-breaker by Kay Thompson, the singer and dancer, during a rehearsal for a nightclub appearance. At a moment when everyone in the room seemed about ready to scream, she changed her voice and announced to the boys in the band, "I am Eloise. I am Six".

The little girl became Kay Thompson's alter ego and by the time her nightclub routine reached The Plaza's Persian Room, Eloise was part of the act.

By 1955 Eloise had become a book and the setting of the book was The Plaza where, according to the storyline, her mother parked her with an English nanny while she flitted around the world looking for other aspects of the good life.

Life at The Plaza was good for a six-year-old. It had mail chutes you could pour water into and elevators you could ride all day. It had wide corridors for tricycle-riding and, best of all, it had room service so that a simple phone call could produce a raisin and seven spoons or a peanut butter and jelly sandwich.

It wasn't long before Eloise became an industry with the licensing of dolls, dresses and bubble gum. There was even an Eloise Easter bonnet created by a top designer for upwardly-mobile six-year-olds.

The Plaza itself became part of the industry. For the first time in its history, the hotel sported children's menus in its restaurants and even established a special soda fountain under the Eloise imprint. Outside they installed a tricycle garage with a fleet of six three-wheelers available free to

Don't look now, but if you're brunching at the Palm Court, America's sweetheart, Eloise, will be looking over your shoulder.

hotel guests (no matter what age), and room left over for others to park their private vehicles for 15 cents a day. Fortunately for the hotel's marble floors, roller skates weren't as popular then as they are now. And just as fortunately for the crystal chandeliers, frisbees hadn't been invented yet.

A great many people believed that Eloise was a real person. A great many others who had spent part of their childhood at The Plaza believed she had been patterned after them. The latter were politely assured that Eloise was entirely fictitious and that any similarity to persons living or dead was purely coincidental. But for the true believers, the hotel kept a room furnished with the proper trappings to make it look like a little girl really lived there. A year after Western International, now known as Westin Hotels, bought The Plaza in 1975, J. Phillip Hughes moved in as its managing director and his young daughter, then five, inherited the Eloise bedspreads and curtains.

But real or not, Eloise was such a hot property that even one of the worst "specials" in the history of television, a spectacular that wasted the talents of Mildred Natwick and Monty Wooley, Charles Ruggles and Ethel

Four other figures watch over you in the Palm Court, too. But don't worry. They've been there since the room had a Tiffany ceiling.

Barrymore couldn't dim her image.

And, thanks to Eloise, even now, almost 30 years later, parents know their children are as welcome at The Plaza as they are. Just about any time.

There was a time in 1964, though, when the staff of The Plaza wished all those kids would go home. But that was like wishing for the wind to stop.

"They seem to be deliberately trying to cause trouble," said the hoarse-voiced Assistant Chief Inspector of Police who was in charge of holding them back. "I think they must be coming here in chartered buses," said a mounted police officer, one of 10 who had the hopeless job of trying to break the mob down into smaller groups.

"We want Beatles! We want Beatles," they shouted over and over again.

John, Paul, George and Ringo had come to New York.

Their manager, Brian Epstein, had been to New York many times and had long before discovered The Plaza. When they scheduled a pair of Carnegie Hall concerts and an appearance on Ed Sullivan's TV show, it was only natural for him to "ring up" The Plaza to give the boys decent digs.

It was reported at the time that The Plaza's reservation office accepted the request for 15 rooms for six days because they had no idea who the Beatles were. It could be true. Some people didn't know them in 1964. But once they appeared in New York, any anonymity they had enjoyed was all over.

A few minutes before the Beatles arrived, Attorney General Robert F. Kennedy appeared at the Fifth Avenue entrance. If anyone recognized him, they didn't acknowledge it. In fact, he had to call for a police escort to get him through the crowd and into the lobby.

Once inside, though, he was given the impression that nothing

The food is as tempting as the setting in The Plaza's Palm Court. It's a perfect place to relax before or after a special party in the State Suite upstairs. (overleaf).

unusual was going on. It was the impression The Plaza wanted him to have. The entire staff had been mobilized to make sure that less-celebrated guests got the service they had a right to expect.

Security had been stepped up to make sure nothing was broken by over-enthusiastic fans, but police barricades outside kept the fans at bay. A few got through, of course. New York youngsters are resourceful. Two girls arrived at the desk with a pair of huge boxes they said were gifts for the Beatles. They were told the boys were out of town for the day and that the packages couldn't be accepted. They didn't quite make it back to the door before the boxes burst open revealing that the "gifts" were two other teenage girls.

Most discovered that the way to break through the security was by

mail or telephone, with the result that The Plaza's mail-room and its telephone room each had the busiest week of its existence. A week they still think of when the going seems to get rough.

But in spite of its potential, the Beatles' week at The Plaza was surprisingly calm. Room service reported an incredible increase in demand for soft drinks, tea and chocolate and the barber shop had a bit of a problem with their hair style. But their Edwardian suits fit right in, and so did they. Best of all, most of the staff was infected with an unusual kind of Beatlemania. You might call it unabashed affection.

From the moment you step into the 59th Street lobby on your way to the Terrace Room or the Ballroom, you have the strong impression that The Plaza was meant to be enjoyed.

The face is familiar

The Plaza staff has been used to entertaining entertainers since the days of Mrs. Patrick Campbell. Until the turn of the century, many hotels flatly refused to accept "show people" as their guests. In those days before computers and credit cards, it was the responsibility of the person at the front desk to determine if a guest might leave without paying. They needed a certain flair for psychology and the criteria they used included sizing up general appearance, quality of clothes and quality of luggage. They generally worked out a series of signals with bellmen to determine if the luggage was full and to find out how the guest arrived at the front door. But for all their tricks, people in the entertainment field were frequently able to outwit them. Fred Sterry had carefully selected seasoned professionals for his hotel and was confident enough to allow theatrical people to stay there.

The Plaza became a theatrical personage herself in fact. In 1930, a film crew pulled up across the street to use the hotel as a backdrop in a scene for *No Limit,* the first talking picture filmed on location in New York City. Its star was the famous "It Girl", Clara Bow. In the years since, film makers and television commercial producers have considered The Plaza "It" when they want to telegraph New York elegance. In at least one case, MGM's blockbuster musical *The Bandwagon,* the hotel was recreated on a Hollywood studio lot. But for films like the recent comedy *Arthur,* producers prefer the real thing even though they are forced to do their work in the wee hours of the morning so the hotel's guests won't be disturbed.

For some films, such as *The Great Gatsby* and *Plaza Suite,* nothing but The Plaza would have worked. For some others like Barbra Streisand's *The Way We Were* and Alfred Hitchcock's *North By Northwest,* the hotel's image on the screen accomplished what dozens of pages of dialogue could never have done.

The Plaza's public relations department carefully studies film scripts and television commercial ideas before giving their permission to put the

hotel on film. Then they work closely with the film crews and the actors to make sure that a tough set of rules are followed to keep the hotel running smoothly in spite of the lights, the cameras, the action.

One thing they don't have to do is help the stars find their way around. The Plaza has always been like a second home to stage and screen luminaries. But of all the show people who have been part of The Plaza's history, only one has a permanent monument there.

He's an American phenomenon named George M. Cohan.

Cohan described himself as a song-and-dance man with strong roots in the vaudevillian tradition. It's what he was, to be sure, but he was much more. He was a songwriter, a producer, a theater owner, a legend. Cohan didn't actually live at The Plaza. In fact, he was one of the people who led the flight to the suburbs when he bought a house in the Westchester community of New Rochelle and wrote a Broadway musical about his experiences "Forty-Five Minutes From Broadway". But if he didn't live at The Plaza, a lot of his fans thought he did because they knew they could see him there just about every day.

The Plaza is less than 10 minutes from Broadway and it was a convenient place for him to unwind after his day in the theater and before the curtain went up on the evening performance. Most days he arrived at

The original Rose restaurant has been matched in elegance by today's Plaza Ballroom.

4.00 and went straight to the northwest corner of the Oak Room where he had a table permanently reserved. His business associates knew where to find him, and from four to seven each day, the Oak Room corner was as important a part of the Broadway scene as Times Square itself.

Some days he was more in a mood for strolling than for planning and reminiscing. When that mood struck him, he went to the cashier's office and bought a roll of quarters, which he dispensed one at a time to folks in Central Park who looked like they could use the money . . . His beneficiaries probably gave him his own curtain line in response: "My mother thanks you, my father thanks you, my sister thanks you . . . and *I* thank you!"

After he died in the early '40s, the Lambs Club put a plaque on the wall and The Plaza officially named the Oak Room's northwest corner "The Cohan Corner." It's a memorial he probably would have loved every bit as much as the statue of himself that was placed in Times Square in just about the same spot that had earlier been proposed for Saint Gaudens' *General Sherman*.

In 1907, a dinner could have a tropical setting (top) or a spring-like atmosphere (right). Today the Ballroom itself is usually considered beautiful enough. But it can still bloom with exotic flowers and trees.

Except in the memories of thousands of people, there is nothing to mark the spot where entertainers built impressive careers and celebrities and socialites competed with each other for attention. For nearly 40 years, it was the place where café society established itself. It was the room at the southeast corner of The Plaza. It was called the Persian Room.

Originally the space had been the hotel's main dining room overlooking 58th Street and the plaza. When the ground floor rooms were juggled around in 1921, it remained a dining room known as the Rose Room. But like so many of New York's dining rooms, it couldn't keep its head above water during the days of Prohibition and the Depression that followed it. The Rose Room quietly went out of existence and was replaced by a showroom for Studebaker automobiles.

But even bad things come to an end, and exactly four months after legal liquor came back, the Rose Room came back, too, rising from the ashes with a new name inspired by a new décor created by Joseph Urban, who had made a name for himself designing sets for the Ziegfeld Follies.

The best part, for many, was the 27-foot bar along the back wall. But the impressive part was a series of five murals by Lillian Palmedo recalling

the festive glory days of the Persian Empire. Urban surrounded them with red velvet drapes and crimson chairs and accented the room with vibrant blue. The Waldorf had its Peacock Alley, but The Plaza had a setting worthy of the Peacock Throne. There was nothing in all New York that quite compared to the Persian Room.

When the supper club opened on April 1, 1934 in a New York Infirmary benefit, it was the first major social event the city had seen since Prohibition was repealed, which made it an event worthy of national attention. Not long after when winter fashions were unveiled (at The Plaza, of course!), the blue color of the room was reflected in just about everything, and no outfit was considered complete without a turban to top it off.

The headliners at the Persian Room on its opening night were Tony and Renee DeMarco, the dance team that brought ballroom dancing out of the closet. They were Persian Room regulars for years. For its formal fall opening that first year, the DeMarcos danced to the music of a young orchestra leader named Eddy Duchin.

Eddy Duchin had already captivated society's younger set with his smile and his syncopated music. But he guaranteed himself a place in their hearts by marrying one of the most glamorous of all the debutantes, Marjorie Oelrichs.

From 1935 until she died in their Plaza apartment a few days after the birth of their son, Peter, in 1937, young Mrs. Duchin entertained her friends while her husband entertained her every night in the Persian Room.

By the time World War II came along, the room was well-established as the best place to hold benefits for war relief or to entertain "our boys." And the person who did it best was the person who appeared more often and for longer periods in the Persian Room than anyone else in its history. Her name was Hildegarde Loretta Sell. She called herself just plain Hildegarde. Press releases called her "The Incomparable Hildegarde."

She really is. She began her career as the only girl in a 12-piece vaudeville orchestra and graduated to the role of accompanist to a varied list of entertainers that included ballplayer Mickey Cochrane and an act called "The Dancing Demarrs," which featured a young Tony DeMarco.

She hit the bigtime by way of London and Paris where she learned to sing in a half-dozen languages and to soft-pedal the German accent she had grown up with in Wisconsin. She also picked up the habit of dressing in the best clothes she could afford and surrounding herself in an air of mystery.

She made it a policy never, ever to mix with her customers on the theory that "if they get to know you too well, they won't pay to see you." The policy paid off in spades in 1934 when the King of Sweden caught her act in Paris and asked that she join him afterward. She told the club's owner she would if she were paid overtime, which of course he agreed to. The encounter was worth a lot more than money as it turned out. It made headlines the next morning, but the Press couldn't figure out if she was Dutch or Viennese or French with an American accent. She left it up to them to figure out.

She was on her way after that. But it took her three years to get back to America. The trip was prompted by a $1,000 a week contract to appear on Ed Wynn's NBC radio program.

She played every major supper club in New York before signing her first six-year contract at the Persian Room. And by then she already had a cult following encouraged by such people as Harriet Van Horne of the *World-Telegram*, who wrote:

"When you see Hildegarde tossing her blond topknot in those pink and golden lights, pinching young soldiers on the cheek and kissing old soldiers

On average, there are as many as eight special events at The Plaza each and every day. They range from small meetings to huge receptions, each and every one a very special occasion.

on their bald spots, she is pure enchantment. You can't forget her playing the piano primly with her gloves on, telling her naughty jokes with the air of a youngster who has been eavesdropping – a chimera in rustling silks, who, you feel sure, goes back to the doll shop when the lights come up."

In 1941, Earl Wilson wrote in the *New York Post* that she was the highest-paid nightclub singer in the world at the time, with an asking price of $2,500 a week and an occasional payoff of twice that. He interviewed her back then in what he called "a 40-acre apartment" in the Savoy-Plaza Hotel. Hildegarde was one of the few entertainers who could work both

sides of the street and still keep everybody happy. She regularly appeared in other New York clubs, but was always more than welcome back home at the Persian Room.

Writing about her salary, columnist Wilson said, "the ash-blonde chanteuse who used to be a piano-pounder in Milwaukee presented this reporter with $468.75 worth of her time, cuffo . . . During a week, Hildegarde will sing 80 minutes a night, six nights a week, which adds up to 480 minutes. Hildegarde works a tough eight-hour week . . . $468.75 worth of her time is exactly an hour and a half."

Of course, in today's terms, it's a low salary for an entertainer who can fill a room twice a night for months on end. Unfortunately, clubs like the Persian Room weren't built with expandable walls and as the cost of

entertainment went up, it got harder and harder to maintain them. Most have become just memories, but the best memories of all are mostly connected with the Persian Room.

It was a culmination of their career for a great many nightclub performers. Barbara McNair said she waited 10 years after her Village Vanguard debut before she felt she was polished enough for The Plaza. It was the beginning of nightclub careers for others. Robert Goulet had three writers working for 18 months, while he himself was appearing on

Sometimes a special meeting can be between two or three people over drinks in the Oak Bar.

Broadway in *Camelot*, before he felt he was ready to make his début at the Persian Room.

After 25 years as a television star, Dinah Shore picked the Persian Room as the place to re-establish herself as a nightclub performer. And Lainie Kazan established herself as something much more than Barbra Streisand's understudy by impressing the Plaza audience.

Generally speaking, the Persian Room was a place to hear singers and to watch dancers. But one week in 1961 just after Hildegarde left town and just before Marguerite Piazza began her engagement, something strange happened.

The New York Times was there and reported:

"The lights are turned down in the posh Persian Room at the stately Plaza hotel. The audience, personifying good manners and gracious living, waits quietly. Into the spotlight steps a tall man with something of a droll

grin. He is impeccably dressed in white tie and tails but he also wears a turban with a purple plume. It is Henny Youngman of Brooklyn, the Borscht Belt and Broadway.

"What does it mean? Is the Persian Room where sophisticated songstresses flourish and not a single lowbrow comedian has passed the maitre d' unless he has paid his way in, diversifying? Is the room looking over the shoulder of bistros from Miami to Las Vegas? Does the move reflect a change in the clientele's taste? Sociologically, is there any significance?"

The Persian Room had rung with laughter before. People like Dorothy Shay, Lisa Kirk and Carol Channing had seen to that. But they were

For years, The Plaza had no identifying sign outside. Today the hotel's name is discreetly displayed on the marquee. But the street that separates it from Grand Army Plaza still has no official name.

musicians. If you discount his fiddle-playing, Henny Youngman represented a serious break with tradition. Another sometime violinist, Jack Benny, once said: "Where I would use three jokes, Bob Hope or Milton Berle would use 12 and Henny Youngman 47."

The audience loved it, by the way. "The reaction to Mr. Youngman's show", said *The Times*, "was neither fury nor shock. The audience liked what it heard. And the applause equaled anything given that long-time Plaza favorite, Hildegarde."

But if they didn't book any other comedians into the Persian Room, the Plaza management realized the need for laughter and responded with PLaza 9-, the room that made satirical sketches the most popular comedy form of the 1960's. To make it work, they hired a young genius named Julius Monk to produce its shows. Monk had been working in New York clubs since 1935 when he signed on as piano player in the bar at One Fifth Avenue. Except for a brief stint in Europe, where he claims to have introduced corn-on-the-cob to Cannes, he's been the personification of a sophisticated New Yorker ever since.

He came to The Plaza's attention as owner of a West 51st Street cabaret called the Downstairs Room. Within two years he had moved five blocks uptown and opened a double-deck club called Upstairs at The Downstairs and Downstairs at The Upstairs. It was only a matter of time before he would go downstairs again at The Plaza.

The Monk formula was disarmingly simple. One critic said his revues

"emphasize cerebral, intimate entertainment. The tone is that of an exceptionally brilliant salon, whose guests have gotten slightly out of hand."

Among the people who began their careers with Monk were Imogene Coca, Jonathan Winters and Tammy Grimes. Tom Jones and Harvey Schmidt and Stephen Sondheim wrote many of the songs and sketches they performed in "basic black" on an otherwise empty stage.

A typical show might have included Nancy Dussault singing a madrigal called "It's a wonderful day to be 17 . . . but I am 22". Or Barbara Minkus discovering a ballad that seems to have been written by Paul

The entrance on The Plaza is called the Fifth Avenue entrance and is most often used. But the main lobby is still on the Park side of the hotel.

McCartney called "Love Letters to My Mother", but turns out to have come from the heart of Warren G. Harding.

The Monk brand of humor is usually called "topical", but once in a while his topics got ahead of the news. Bill Dana did a PLaza 9-sketch on cigarettes and cancer a full six years before the surgeon general determined that cigarette smoking is dangerous to your health. Sometimes they got ahead of the audience. Monk did a number on discotheques in the early '60s, but had to take it out of the show because his audience didn't know what a disco was.

Politicians were grist for his mill. When Senator Barry Goldwater was running for president, they rolled out a number about "The Losing Generation." The Senator came back three times to catch every nuance. When they did a calypso song about First Lady Jacqueline Kennedy called "The Jackie Look," ("Learn to sew, learn to cook, learn to read Portuguese from a book . . .") Monk got a letter from the White House. Not a cease-and-desist note, but an invitation to perform there.

When he was Senator, John F. Kennedy was impressed by a Monk parody called "Presidential Spectacular." He asked for a copy of the script, which he and his wife, along with Mr. and Mrs. Peter Lawford performed for his father at the family retreat in Hyannis, Mass.

The elder Kennedy may well have seen the original cast production at The Plaza. The hotel was one of his favorite New York addresses and the place where his children first felt New York's brand of excitement.

Presidential families have been part of the Plaza scene since the Roosevelts . . . the Theodore Roosevelts, that is. T.R. was in the White House when the hotel opened, and was hard at work at the time promoting the cause of his successor, William Howard Taft. By tradition, Republican politics in New York had been centered at the Fifth Avenue Hotel on Madison Square. The "boss of all bosses," Senator Thomas C. Platt, dispensed favors and patronage and gave marching orders to the party faithful there every Sunday afternoon with the gathering of what he called

his Sunday school in a part of the hotel dining room the Press called the "Amen Corner." Within six months of The Plaza's opening, the Fifth Avenue Hotel closed, leaving the Grand Old Party without a base. The President quietly moved them up the street where their wheeling and dealing went on in a more genteel way at The Plaza.

Once he successfully got Taft elected, Roosevelt retired and came back home to New York to keep an eye on things. When he wanted to be in the public eye, which was most of the time, he often chose The Plaza as the place to be. It was also the place he chose to meet with local people who might support him in his bid to keep the Taft administration down to one term by running against him as the candidate of the Bull Moose Party.

In spite of the fact that their friendship had deteriorated, Taft ran the risk of meeting the former president time and again by making it a point to

Taking the stairs to the Terrace Room or an elevator to one of the guest suites (opposite page and overleaf) is especially rewarding because of what you find at the end of the trip.

visit The Plaza just about every time he came to New York. It was worth the risk. He liked the place. He liked it so much, he encouraged his son and daughter-in-law to become permanent residents. And that gave him a convenient New York base after he was forced into retirement.

It was Harry S. Truman's daughter, Margaret, who introduced him to The Plaza, and it became a favorite place for them to meet for good food and quiet conversation whenever he was in New York.

When Richard Nixon lived nearby on Fifth Avenue, the Edwardian Room was almost his second home and it was the first place he and his wife went the day he conceded the Presidential Election to John F. Kennedy in 1960. The hotel was also the scene of a happier occasion in his life, his daughter's wedding reception in the Plaza Ballroom.

Presidents, princes and potentates have been adding to The Plaza atmosphere since the day in 1907 when the personal representative of the last Emperor of China was carried through the front door on a litter followed by a retinue of servants. He was pleased to see his country's flag over the door, a gesture that had been the brainchild of Fred Sterry and a tough assignment, indeed, for the staff member dispatched to find a big Chinese flag.

It's a problem that has long since been solved by keeping a supply of flags on hand to honor important foreign guests. In 1925, though, an unexpected problem came up when the Italian and French Ambassadors showed up at the same time as the Minister from Sweden and the President-elect of Cuba. The hotel had all the right flags but only four flagpoles. The solution was to add a fifth to accommodate the American flag.

Not every problem involving VIP guests is as easily solved, but all of them are usually solved smoothly at The Plaza. When the King of Morocco arrived he never knew that a member of the housekeeping staff had just left the room he had reserved with a huge bouquet of carnations she noticed

there in her last-minute check. She knew what the florist didn't know, that carnations are flowers for the dead in Morocco.

When the president of a South American country was a Plaza guest, a military attaché sent his leader's laundry out to be done. It was done quickly, as requested. The Plaza is one of the few hotels anywhere in the United States with its own laundry. But when it was delivered, every piece of presidential underwear had been marked with the young lieutenant's name. Fortunately, the president had a sense of humor and calmed his aide by pointing out that he now had a daily reminder of his young aide's efficiency.

Not every national leader is that understanding. Some Plaza bellmen still turn ashen when they are reminded of the night a prince arrived from the East with his entire retinue, each with an impressive collection of

The pointed spire of the Sherry-Netherland Hotel and the French-inspired roof of the Pierre Hotel are a perfect complement to The Plaza's Fifth Avenue facade.

They're a beautiful part of the most beautiful skyline in the world (opposite page, and overleaf).

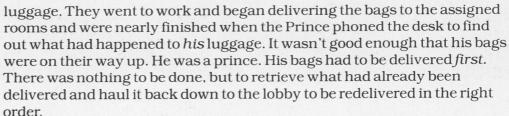

luggage. They went to work and began delivering the bags to the assigned rooms and were nearly finished when the Prince phoned the desk to find out what had happened to *his* luggage. It wasn't good enough that his bags were on their way up. He was a prince. His bags had to be delivered *first*. There was nothing to be done, but to retrieve what had already been delivered and haul it back down to the lobby to be redelivered in the right order.

Ici on parle 'New York'

Some years ago, the late Lucius Beebe, who built a career as the chronicler of the good life, said of The Plaza:

"From the very beginning it was an institution, and the legend of its being richly upholstered in the manners and possessions of the wealthy and celebrated of the world has continued in unabated magnificence from that time right down to the immediate here and now."

It continues still. People who sponsor society benefits and balls, fashion shows and debutante parties consider themselves lucky to get onto The Plaza's crowded calendar which averages six to eight special functions each and every day.

Each and every one of those functions is an event that continues the Plaza legend. Occasionally they add to it. Back in the 1950s, when men were beginning to grumble about having to wear neckties to formal parties, The Plaza began allowing them to appear in turtle-neck shirts, a fashion idea that swept the country overnight. At the same time young debutantes began rebelling against curtsying on receiving lines. It became acceptable to substitute a handshake at Plaza coming-out parties with the result that there are very few young American girls today who have any idea what a

curtsy is.

The first party at The Plaza was in honor of the Lord Bishop of London two weeks after the hotel opened. Possibly the most talked-about was Truman Capote's 1966 Black and White Ball which was held there, according to the writer, because "The Plaza has the only truly beautiful ballroom left in New York."

It was called the party of the century, and it may well have been exactly that. Capote called it "a little masked ball for Kay Graham and all my friends." His list of friends included politicians and scientists, writers and actors, social lions and business tycoons as well as "international types, lots of beautiful women and ravishing little things." He invited 540 of them to honor Mrs. Philip L. Graham, president of the *Washington Post*. People who weren't invited made it a point to be out of town on the big night, others simply lied, confident no one would notice that they weren't there.

They were found out the next morning when Charlotte Curtis published the entire guest list along with her story on the party in *The Times*. In her book, "The Rich and Other Atrocities," she said:

"The list itself was as much the news the next morning as the coverage of the party, and telephones rang all along the party circuit about who was and who wasn't included.... In journalistic circles, the big question was how *The Times* got the list. Suffice it to say that Truman did not give us the list, that we did not steal it, that we had it in type before the party began, and that I copied each and every one of the 540 names down in longhand."

In an earlier era, the list of who was important in New York society was limited to 400, the capacity of Mrs. Astor's ballroom. But this was 1966 and America had outgrown such things. Still, the list was a spectacular one.

The Oyster Bar is a relatively new Plaza tradition, but no less impressive for its newness. It was built in a space formerly occupied by a drug store.

The invitations had requested that men wear dinner jackets and black masks. Women were given their choice of black or white dresses, but their masks should be white. Capote himself showed up in a mask he had picked up across the street in the F.A.O. Schwartz toy store for 39 cents, but some guests were said to have spent as much as $600 for feathers and rhinestones to cover their faces. Mrs. Joseph P. Kennedy bought several masks in case she changed her mind; H. J. Heinz II, who flew in from Pittsburgh to be there, made his own from a paper plate.

The host had requested masks because he thought it was a romantic idea. "The whole point is to ask anyone you want to dance and sit wherever you want and then when the masks come off at midnight, you can find your old chums or stay with your new ones."

In spite of the disguises, finding the right people was no problem. The most popular table was the one that included Frank Sinatra and Claudette Colbert, followed closely by another where guests looking for new chums could chat with Lynda Bird Johnson, the president's daughter, or Wendy Vanderbilt, daughter of The Plaza's first guest.

An important party? Of course. But, as they say, nothing unimportant ever happens at The Plaza, and every wedding, ball and board of directors meeting is considered a main event.

The one many New Yorkers remember most fondly took place in 1968 in playwright Neil Simon's imagination. It was a Broadway production called "Plaza Suite," a show critic Clive Barnes said "will set the whole town laughing." He was right, it did.

The laughs were generated by three different groups of fictional people who occupied the same suite at The Plaza at different times. One was the distraught parents of a bride who had locked herself in the bathroom while wedding guests were downstairs in the Baroque Suite enjoying themselves at her father's expense, another was a businessman with designs on his secretary and the third was an aging film producer who lured his childhood sweetheart, also aging, to The Plaza to show her what he'd learned about seduction.

A lot of things at The Plaza were once something else. Trader Vic's is on the site of the former barber shop; the Fifth Avenue lobby was once a dining room. But the Oak Room is an original. It was the architect's favorite room, in fact.

Interestingly, Simon's creations were not the out-of-towners who would usually populate a play about a hotel, they were all New Yorkers.

New Yorkers take a special interest in The Plaza. It's where they prefer to celebrate the marriages of their daughters as well as other family occasions, and it's where they go to commemorate such milestones of life as birthdays and anniversaries. It's a favorite place for intracity vacations, too, and it's not at all unusual for The Plaza's guest register to include dozens of Manhattanites on weekends when special rates are in effect.

Any Sunday at all, the accents you hear during brunch in the Palm Court are as often home-grown as any other. But one Sunday every year, it

seems as though all New York turns up. The Plaza, you see, is the ultimate destination of Fifth Avenue's Easter Parade.

The annual march began back in the days of the old Plaza when it became customary for worshippers from St. Thomas Church and from St. Patrick's Cathedral to stroll past the half-mile of mansions that lined the Avenue from the cathedral to the park. The hotel became a natural

Through the etched glass doors of the Oyster Bar pass the freshest seafood and most satisfied seafood lovers in the City of New York.

stopping-off point for a little refreshment after all that walking. The tradition has grown, if anything, and the Palm Court is expanded to include the Terrace Room on that one day to accommodate the paraders.

Occasionally, New Yorkers take a leaf from F. Scott Fitzgerald's book and, like *The Great Gatsby,* drop around to The Plaza for quiet relaxation and serious conversation. Jay Gatsby and his friends preferred to rent the parlor or a suite, but modern New Yorkers often choose The Plaza's Oyster Bar, a restaurant that looks for all the world like it has been dispensing its famous Crab Meat Remick since the day the hotel opened, in spite of the fact it's The Plaza's newest restaurant on the site of the old employee cafeteria.

When New Yorkers are in a mood for celebrity-watching (which is more often than their reputation for being blasé suggests), they go downstairs at The Plaza into another world, a world called Trader Vic's. It's

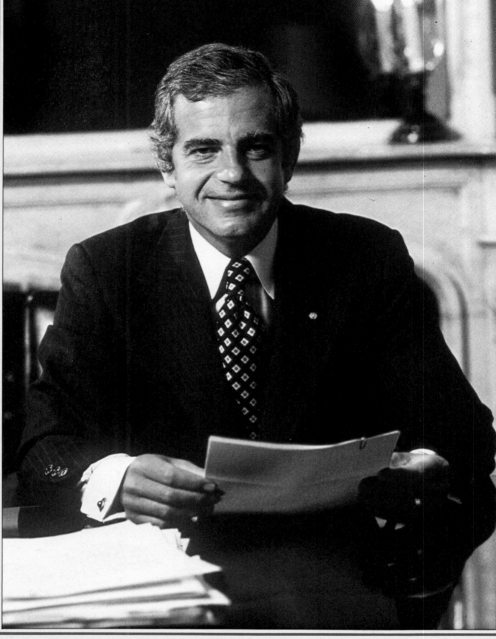

The job of keeping The Plaza in tune with the times but never out of touch with the past belongs to J. Philip Hughes, the hotel's managing director.

a favorite haunt of politicians and show people, especially Hollywood show people who seem to go there to fight off homesickness for California.

The Trader himself is a flamboyant Californian named Victor J. Bergeron who gave up a car-parts business to open a chophouse in Oakland in 1934. He gave the restaurant a South Seas décor to attract attention and attracted so much of it, he was forced to change his menu to match the decorations.

By the time his chain had expanded across the country as far as New York, the décor and the menu had become both sophisticated and exotic. Most of the artifacts hanging from the ceilings and the walls were gathered by his network of real traders operating from Africa to Tahiti with instructions to collect recipes as well. What had to be created on the spot was carefully researched, and the contractor who installed it was even forced to hire an able seaman to make certain that all the nautical touches were ship-shape and Bristol-fashion.

When the first fire was lit in the restaurant's Chinese smoke ovens, the

sailor presumably went back to sea. But if there are no sailors on The Plaza's payroll today, there are some fairly exotic job descriptions there. The hotel's staff includes silversmiths, furniture restorers, upholsterers and crystal polishers. The kitchen staff includes the expected cake decorators, chicken boners and chefs with specialties ranging from soup to walnut cake, but it also includes ice sculptors who can whip up a frozen tribute to the guest of honor at any kind of party.

It wouldn't be completely honest to say that The Plaza has never kept a seaman on its payroll. Back in 1907, the hotel pioneered the idea of toll-free reservations by advertising that it would accept collect wireless messages from ships at sea bound for New York. Then as the liners approached Ambrose Light they were met by a small boat dispatched by The Plaza with a special agent who took it on himself to make sure they went through customs with a minimum of fuss and that their luggage was delivered to the right hotel.

The Plaza has been going out of its way to welcome foreign visitors ever since. More than 80 percent of the staff is multilingual, speaking more than 35 different languages from Arabic to several Slavic tongues, and they all get plenty of practice. For international businessmen, the hotel provides 24-hour Telex service to allow them to reach any spot in the world with

their messages translated for them into the local language.

But for all its Old-World interest, The Plaza is what New Yorkers like to think their city is all about. It abounds in superlatives. It takes an army of 1300 people to keep it running smoothly, most of whom are quick to tell you they couldn't imagine working anywhere else (some of whom never have!). It houses five restaurants under a single roof and provides room service 24 hours a day. It consumes 1500 pounds of prime rib every week along with 1300 pounds of filet, 850 pounds of bacon and 1700 dozen eggs, not to mention 1100 pounds of butter just for cooking. Its on-premises laundry washes 33 tons of linen every month, and its bill for heat, electricity and gas makes it the utility company's second or third biggest customer.

But what native New Yorkers like best is that the more The Plaza changes, the more it stays the same. It's one of the very few 75-year-old buildings in town still used for the same purpose its builders intended.

The original backers were involved in running the hotel through good times and bad for the rest of their lives. In 1930, Harry Black, who had built himself an opulent penthouse on The Plaza's roof, became one of the first suicides in the oncoming Great Depression. Two years later, Ben Beinecke, then 87, died peacefully in his Plaza apartment. Then within a few months, Fred Sterry also died.

Sterry had become president of the Plaza Operating Company, which had built the Savoy-Plaza Hotel across Fifth Avenue in 1927 and was running both hotels at the time of his death.

Beinecke's sons, whose interests include the Sperry-Hutchinson company which made "Green Stamps" a national institution, kept the company together during the Depression and into World War II, but were forced to put The Plaza on the market in 1943. The buyer was Conrad Hilton, who considered the acquisition the crowning point of one of the most impressive careers any hotel man has ever boasted. He lavished love on The Plaza for 10 years before selling it to Boston industrialist A. M. Sonnabend in 1953. The Sonnabend family kept the legend alive from then until 1975 when they announced that The Plaza was for sale.

There had been rumors of such a sale for weeks and hotel people around the world were eager to participate. But the actual announcement was made on a Saturday and it was made clear that the deal would have to be completed before the weekend was over.

Out in Seattle, Washington, an executive of Western International Hotels, Harry Mullikin, put together a team of negotiators, a job that involved having one of his fellow executives paged at a football game, and headed for New York. When they got there, their only competition was a team from a British-based hotel firm. But they proved to be tough competitors and negotiations continued through the night and well into Sunday. Finally a firm price was established, but it proved to be slightly higher than the British team had come prepared to pay. They were sure they could come up with the extra money, but had to beg for time because they needed to consult with the chairman of their company who they knew was out on his yacht that afternoon. They didn't want to bother him, they said, and asked to postpone the final sale until Monday morning.

By Monday morning, though, the papers had been signed and the price ... $25 million for the hotel and $2 million for the land under it ... had been paid. The British firm had lost the opportunity. It is mercifully unrecorded what their chairman had to say when his ship came in.

Western International was already well-steeped in the tradition that comes with the address at 59th and Fifth. They had owned the Savoy-Plaza until it was demolished to make way for the General Motors Building.

The company, whose name was changed to Westin Hotels in 1981,

Of all the things that make The Plaza beautiful, the most beautiful of all is the smiling faces of people who find so much to enjoy there.

(and whose president and chief executive officer today is the same Harry Mullikin who bought the Plaza), owns or operates 55 hotels and resorts in 14 countries including places as exotic as Singapore and as difficult to pronounce as Ixtapa-Zihuatanejo on Mexico's Pacific coast.

Its first move on acquiring The Plaza was to begin restoring it, and to do the job they moved J. Phillip Hughes, manager of their Hotel Scandinavia in Copenhagen from there to New York. He's been managing director of The Plaza ever since and from the day he arrived construction work hasn't stopped. Elevators have been refurbished, air conditioning improved. New carpeting has been installed, telephone service modernized, plumbing replaced, furniture and architectural detail restored. Every guest room has been renovated and, like the painting of the George Washington Bridge, once the painters finished the last room they went back to the first and started all over again. The budget for all this is over $8 million a year with no letup in sight.

But through it all, the goal has always been to make the modernization something you feel rather than see. The commitment is to keep The Plaza the way it was and still make it work. "We think it's a very New Yorkerish hotel," says Phil Hughes. "We think that is very right."

A lot of New Yorkers agree.

In her column on architecture in *The New York Times*, Ada Louise Huxtable, a person who takes a back seat to no one in her love for New York, once wrote:

"Growing up in New York with teas at The Plaza from a very early age, my appreciation of the past and even my feeling for New York is undoubtedly conditioned by association with that solid structure. I did not learn until years after those teas that the architect was Henry J. Hardenbergh and the date of its construction was 1907, and that it was the high point of Edwardian design, inside and out.

"I thought it had been there forever and was something absolute."

Anyone who has ever looked out of a Plaza window and seen Central Park in the twilight and listened to the sound of horses' hooves or walked through the Fifth Avenue entrance in the evening and heard the sounds of traffic turn to the strains of a violin gets the same feeling.

The Plaza is something absolute. The Plaza is New York.

Published in 1981 by Poplar Books Inc.,
a division of Book Sales Inc.,
110 Enterprise Avenue,
Secaucus, New Jersey 07094
© 1981 Illustrations and text: Colour Library International Ltd.,
New Malden, Surrey, England.
Colour separations by FER-CROM, Barcelona, Spain.
Display and text filmsetting by The Printed Word, London, England
Printed and bound by JISA-RIEUSSET, Barcelona, Spain
ISBN 0-89009-525-6
COLOUR LIBRARY INTERNATIONAL

WESTIN HOTELS

The Plaza

The Plaza Hotel
is owned by the New York Westin Hotel Company